DON'T TELL ME I CAN'T

THE TRIUMPHANT STORY OF A THALIDOMIDE SURVIVOR

A Book Republic Production

Published in 2011 by Book Republic, an imprint of Maverick House
Publishers.
Office 19, Dunboyne Business Park, Dunboyne, Co. Meath, Ireland.

www.bookrepublic.ie
email: info@bookrepublic.ie

ISBN 978-1-907221-28-6

10 9 8 7 6 5 4 3 2 1

The paper used in this book comes from wood pulp of managed
forests. For every tree felled, at least one tree is planted, thereby
renewing natural resources.

A CIP catalogue record for this book is available from the British
Library.

DON'T TELL ME I CAN'T

THE TRIUMPHANT STORY OF A THALIDOMIDE SURVIVOR

LEIGH GATH

BOOK REPUBLIC

A BOUTIQUE PUBLISHING PRESS

For my sister Anne, the strongest and most

dignified woman I've known.

Acknowledgements

My mother, for believing in me and raising me to be the woman I am today.

My husband Eugene, for all his love and support.

Karl and Aisling, for allowing me to include them even though their friends will read the book.

Lura Taheri, for encouraging me to write the book in the first place.

My sister, Anne Rice, who passed away recently but was always there to teach me and to listen.

Chrstina O'Dwyer and Tina Nunan—without them I could not lead an independent life.

Contents

Foreword

In 1954, a small chemical company in Germany synthesised a new chemical by the name of phthalimidoglutarimide. This name was shortened to thalidomide. It was to be used as a mild sedative and was deemed safe for use by pregnant women. It was seen as an exciting new alternative to barbiturates, which were sometimes taken with alcohol by people committing suicide. But who would have guessed that 15 years later the name thalidomide would forever be associated with changing so many lives.

By 1957 the drug was being widely distributed and used in over 40 countries. It was similarly used as a sedative, but many doctors were giving it to their pregnant patients to help combat morning sickness. The theory behind this seemed to be that if the woman was sleeping she couldn't be nauseous. Back then drugs were not thoroughly tested as they are today and many governments took it as a given that the German chemical company had thoroughly tested the drug, so they did not bother to run their own tests. The exception to this was the USA, where the Food and Drug Administration was still carrying out its own research when the news broke about the drug being responsible for birth defects in tens of thousands of babies all over the world. In the UK doctors were assured by the British Government at the time, that this new 'wonder drug' was safe for pregnant women and many doctors were encouraged to give it to their patients, some even gave it to their own pregnant wives to help them through the sickness experienced in the first trimester of pregnancy.

By 1961 all was not going well with thalidomide. Children were being born with many birth defects such as stunted or missing limbs; missing or malformed fingers, thumbs and toes; no ears; blind, deaf and some with internal organ damage. Many more children died before birth or were stillborn with similar birth defects. It is estimated that only about 40% of the affected children survived birth, with more dying before their fifth birthday because of the damage thalidomide had done to them in uterus.

Thalidomide was withdrawn from the market towards the end of 1961 after a Dr McBride from Australia realized the link between his own patients having babies with birth defects and the woman taking thalidomide. By this time it had been taken by pregnant women in Europe, Japan, Australia, New Zealand, Canada and other countries throughout the world. Tens of thousands of children had been born with disabilities by then. The first child was born in Germany in December 1956 but it took another four years for the company to conclusively draw a link with thalidomide. Then it even some more time for governments to act and withdraw the drug from sale.

Although a notice was sent to pharmacies and doctors to stop using the drug because it was being recalled, no notice was given to the public. This meant that women who had been given the drug at an earlier time didn't realize its potential to harm the foetus and it was months before the public were made aware of the consequences of taking thalidomide.

My mother, living in Northern Ireland, had already taken the drug, licensed in the UK under the name of Distaval. She told me that she only ever took three pills, three days in a row. She was around two months pregnant with me at the time and was so incredibly sick she found it difficult to even keep down water. She told me the pills made her feel sleepy and out of control and so, with two young girls to look after, she threw the rest away. Because she had taken the pills during an important time of growth of the fetus, I was poisoned in the womb and my limbs were affected.

I have no shoulder sockets, arms that are around eight inches long, with no elbow joint or proper wrist joint. I have three fingers all functional on my left hand and four fingers with two of them functional on my right hand. The other two fingers are stuck together. I have no hip sockets and my legs are about six inches long. My feet are turned upside down. I have five toes on each foot but my big toes did not grow and so they are the smallest toes.

When I was born my parents were told I would always need care and would never be independent. They were also told I would probably not live very long. Despite these low expectations for me, I have lived an amazing life. I wanted to write this book so that other people facing adversity in their lives might understand that only you should have the power to decide what kind of life you lead.

After a lengthy court battle when I was around ten years old, where compensation was based on a short life expectancy, the Thalidomide Trust was established. There were 450 survivors in the UK and Northern Ireland who could benefit from this Trust. However, until recent years any money given to survivors from the Trust was taxed at the highest rate by the British Government. The compensation given to survivors may seem like a lot, but it really was a pittance when one considers the cost of disability. For example, a powered wheelchair costs roughly €20,000 and needs to be replaced every three or four years, a car can cost up to €80,000 just to be functional for some people and needs to be replaced every five or so years, the cost of modifying a home just to make it accessible can cost thousands of euro, and clothes alterations to suit strangely shaped bodies also costs a fortune.

As I age, my body is beginning to let me down through overuse. I now have major neck and shoulder pain caused by having to pick my children up with my teeth when they were babies, and following surgery for cancer my arms have lost some strength. But if one were to dwell on the negative side of life, then an opportunity would be wasted to take every opportunity that life gives, the opportunity to live every day to the full.

At the beginning of 2010, the British Government made an attempt at an apology for allowing the use of thalidomide in the UK. They also added some compensation money to the thalidomide pot to help ease the burden of aging bodies and more expensive equipment needed to keep people independent. However, seemingly to add insult to injury, the apology was not even offered by the Prime Minister and was given by a Minister to an almost empty House of Commons. It appears that, even after 50 years, the Government would be happy to put this chapter of history behind them.

It has to be said, if it were not for a small group of extremely dedicated thalidomide survivors from the UK, there would have been no apology or extra money. They worked tirelessly with MPs for some years to educate them on thalidomide and have them fulfil their responsibilities. The Irish survivors are still fighting for justice.

IN THE BEGINNING

I WAS BORN IN DAISY HILL HOSPITAL, NEWRY, Northern Ireland in April 1962. I was born a 'thalidomide baby'—both my arms and legs were deformed. Although I have a bone in both my arms I have no shoulder joints as the socket did not form, so instead I have an arm bone with a ball on the top with nothing to slot into, so it's free moving. I have no hip joints, again the socket did not form and so again the bones move freely. My pelvis is a weird shape too. My legs are about six inches long from hip to the end and my feet are turned upside down. My toes are in the correct order but my big toe on both feet is tiny and neither of my big toes have a bone in them.

My mother, during her early stages of pregnancy with me was not able to keep down food or water so the doctors prescribed a new drug—thalidomide. She took the first pill one day when she had my sisters in the park and according to her, just about made it home with them before collapsing into bed. She followed the doctor's instructions and over the next two days took two more pills, but they made her feel so bad that she threw the rest away. As her pregnancy went into the second trimester she felt better so she soon forgot all about those little pills.

Several weeks before my birth the midwife, during a routine examination, could not feel any arms or legs, so my mother was advised to rest during the rest of her pregnancy. The doctors thought that I was just sitting in an awkward position—at the time there were no scans/ultrasounds.

I was one of 12 children born with birth defects in what was then a country-type hospital and within a relatively short space of time doctors began to question what could have caused such a rash of birth defects. It wasn't long before the link became apparent—all the mothers had taken thalidomide during pregnancy.

The doctors at the hospital told my parents that I would need to be constantly looked after, so they should put me into care and go home and try again. Their diagnosis was that I would never sit unaided because I had no hip joints and my legs would not be long enough to support me or move unaided. They stated that I would not be able to feed, dress, or use the toilet by myself because I had no shoulder joints and my arms were so short. According to my late mother, she was told I would need round the clock care for the rest of my life. She was also told I probably would not live beyond 18 years old. I have proved those doctors wrong on so many levels.

My mother and father were working class people who treated me just the same as my sisters had been when they were babies, although there were numerous hospital visits because, although my health was very good, the doctors were keen to see what progress we would make in our development compared to other children our age. Thalidomide kids were a whole new medical concept and the doctors were keen to learn as much as possible from us.

My sister Anne, who was older than me, would prop me in a sitting position with cushions all around me. This strengthened my back and leg muscles and although she didn't realise it at the time, was starting me out on the road to independence. She also taught me how to feed myself later by buying an ice cream cone and making me hold it and eat it. Of course, like all toddlers, most of it ended up around me than in me. But at least now my mother knew that the expectations doctors had for me were wrong, and that I was capable of learning how to do things for myself.

At the age of two I was sent two days a week to a nursery school in Belfast for children affected by thalidomide. Being so young, it was all play to me. But it was here I was observed using my arms and little legs, how I could shuffle around on my butt, play with other kids, and it was here I was fitted with my first pair of artificial legs. However, the artificial legs never felt like a part of me and I was much more able without them. My first little legs had sockets made of leather that my own legs would be laced into from my hips right down to my toes, with my legs forced to stretch straighter than they were normally. Then there was a little artificial leg fitted on beneath with a little foot that I could fit shoes onto. The physiotherapist bought me a toy dog on wheels for my third birthday and I learned to walk pushing the dog along. I also had a circular, cage-like contraption with six castor wheels at equal intervals attached to the bottom of it. I was put inside and walked holding onto the top of it which was heavily padded – a little like the baby walkers of today. But this was taken off me when I learnt how to put one foot up on the bottom bar and push along with the other. Once I had built up some speed I would put the other foot up too. It was fun until I tipped over and would come crashing face first to the ground. After my first tumble I was made to wear a rubbery helmet that hit the ground first when I toppled over, protecting my head. My arms were too short to be of any use when I fell.

I have memories of the little nursery school. In the bathroom was a set of steps, spaced well apart. Those of us without legs would climb these little steps so we could reach the sink from the top one to wash our hands before lunch. I also remember being put down for a nap on a type of camping cot. I never did like nap time because there was so much fun stuff to do—who wanted to sleep?

I'm at 'Big' School Now

I SPENT MY FIRST COUPLE OF YEARS OF LIFE LIVING in a terrace house on a street in Newry in Northern Ireland. As was common back then, people would leave their front doors open and so I would crawl out of our house and into the houses next door to us. On one side there was a convent, and apparently I would go and knock on their front door. The nuns thought this was very cute and they would take me inside. When it was time to go home I would always be carried back holding sweets or biscuits or some other nice treat. As my dad had died when I was two years old, there was no money to spare for treats and so the nuns' gifts were always welcome. The house that we lived in was eventually condemned by the local authorities and when I was four years old we moved to a brand new housing estate that was being built on the outskirts of town.

When I was little more than a toddler, one of the nuns would, on occasion, take me into her classroom and sit me on her desk to play. But even though I was brought to the school by her, the local schools felt they could not deal with a kid like me simply because in the 1960s schools were full of stairs, steps, and children moving from class to class all the time, so I was sent away to a 'special' school in Belfast. The journey would have taken over an hour each way because the roads were of poor quality, so I had to board at the school from Sunday to Friday, coming home at the weekends. This school was set up to educate children with physical disabilities, but until the arrival of the 'thalidomide kids' the level of formal education was lower than regular schools. Back then many people had low or no expectations that kids with disabilities would grow up to become working, tax paying citizens, enjoying the same lifestyles as their non-disabled counterparts. However, now the education system had to deal with kids of average or higher IQ who could not attend regular schools because of access, and needed physio and occupational therapy. So the decision was made to send all of us who needed a 'special' school to Fleming Fulton school in Belfast. Some of the children affected by thalidomide were able to attend their local schools because their disabilities were not as severe as mine.

I began school in 1967 when I was five years old.

As well as having regular classes I was taught by the occupational therapists how to dress and go to the toilet by myself. I also got my first wheelchair that I could move independently. Before I got the chair I would simply roll from class to class in the school, or hop sideways along the ground. I was quite fast at both. The wheelchair was designed with the seat very low and the back wheels larger than normal so that I could reach them with my little arms. I could push the chair on flat ground, but I couldn't get up hills or stop myself when I was going down a steep incline. One time I let go of the wheels at the top of a small hill and only came to a stop at the bottom when the chair hit a kerb. Now I know what it feels like to be fired out of a cannon.

I made lots of friends at school and enjoyed being there. Boarding at the school and living away from home began to make me more independent as a person and able to think for myself at a young age. But it also had its drawbacks. As time passed, the children back at home became used to me not being around and so I had to learn to try to fit in again each time I went home. That was difficult because I grew to have less and less in common with the kids in Newry—they didn't know my friends or teachers from school and I didn't know theirs. Funny things that happened to them meant nothing to me because I didn't know a lot of the people involved, and vice versa.

The boarding part of the school had a large living area. One half had carpet and that is where the huge stone fireplace and television were. The other side of the room had a wooden floor, which was the part where we ate. One night one of the staff was carrying me into the room from the kitchen when her foot caught on a rolled up edge of the carpet. Both of us went flying and I came down, hitting the side of my head on a table. My ear was practically torn off and there was blood everywhere. An ambulance was called and I was taken to the Royal Victoria Hospital to be stitched up. Unfortunately this happened during the time of the Troubles and there was rioting every night in Belfast. I vividly remember lying in the back of the ambulance hearing the stones thud off it as we drove along the Falls Road into the hospital. That was more scary than the stitches.

By the time I was ten the British Army had moved into Northern Ireland. Some began coming to the boarding part of the school in the evenings, and they were lots of fun. They would arrive in one of their jeeps and park it way out of sight so that it could not be seen from the road. A few of the soldiers had begun dating some of the staff, and they would come visit us but be able to spend time with their girlfriend as well.

One Christmas they threw a huge Christmas party for the boarders at the school. There was a mountain of food and soft drinks, and each one of us got a Christmas present. I got a diary with a lock and key, and I thought this was the most amazing present ever for me. All teenage girls have their little secrets—secret crushes on guys, who you like or don't like—and to be able to write down all these things and keep them locked was great.

There were other Christmas parties thrown for us by different charities but the one I always enjoyed most was the one held at the Crawfordsburn Inn—where of course Santa would come and give everyone gifts. We were allowed to run amok in this bar/restaurant for the afternoon, fuelled with lots of sweet food and fizzy drinks.

Because we were a single parent family I didn't get many presents for Christmas most years at home. There just wasn't much money available. In fact I remember one Christmas we got no presents, and we had sausages for Christmas dinner instead of turkey. I was six at the time, and that is when I was told there would be no Santa this year. I cried for hours, not understanding what I'd done that was so wrong that I got no presents. I was completely broken hearted.

WE ENJOYED THE SOLDIERS COMING OVER TO THE school, but I couldn't mention it when I went home because we lived in a very Republican Catholic area, and even at that tender young age I knew that it could have put all of us at risk if it was known they were going to the school regularly.

One night we were lying in bed at the school and we heard a noise outside. I was about 10 or 11 years old. I shared a room with three other girls and we were lying awake chatting. We put on the light and opened the curtains a bit to look at what was happening at the shops across the road. There were flashing lights and shouts. Next thing, police officers and soldiers began running towards the school. Our bedroom door burst open and we were all lifted out of bed and carried to the other side of the building. There was a bomb in the shops and the police hadn't realized anyone was in the school until they saw the curtains moving and the light. Less than five minutes after we were moved, the bomb exploded. The windows had already been covered in heavy tape so if they came in it would be in large pieces.

Bombs and shootings were a way of life. For much of the mid-70's, when the Troubles were really bad in Belfast, children from the troubled areas would come to school and be put to lie down on cots to sleep. They would have been up all night listening to the rioting and shooting taking place outside their windows.

We were all affected by the Troubles, some more than others. A friend of mine had a brother who was playing with a mate upstairs in the family area of a pub, when a bomb went off in the bar downstairs. He was killed. We also had one or two children come to the school who were themselves the victims of explosions, resulting in disabilities. But having lived with the Troubles most of my young life, I thought this was the way of the world and everyone lived like this. My mom used to tell me that if I went into town with her I would not let her pass a car that was parked strangely on the pavement in case it blew up when we were passing.

BY THE TIME I HAD REACHED TWELVE YEARS OLD I decided to stop wearing artificial legs. In order for the sockets to be made for the legs I would have had to have plaster casts taken of my legs right up to my hips so that my weight would sit on the socket and take most of the weight off my legs and feet. As I began to develop as a teenager I was very self conscious of having these moulds taken. I never liked how the legs felt and they didn't look natural when I walked, so I decided that I could function just as well, or better, without them. Because my own legs were so short I had to walk stiff legged—a little Frankenstein himself in the movies.

I found over the years that I could balance on my own legs even though I was walking on my ankle bone because my feet are upside down. The physio department at the school gave me little crutches and I flew around the school using them. However, I couldn't go outside in bare feet so a little pair of bootees were designed for me—they were made from a mold of my legs and were soft on the inside and hard plastic on the outside. But I wore those out in about a week. So another pair was designed with a tough fibreglass-type exterior and rubber soles. The soles were flat and gave me such good balance I didn't need to use the crutches any more. The doctors could never understand how I balanced because I don't actually have any hip joints. Although I was only 3ft 4 inches standing up, walking meant that now I could get into buildings with steps. The designer of my little boots added 3-4 inches on the bottom to give me a little extra height. Although I could walk and run in the boots, I still needed a wheelchair for longer distances, but walking allowed me the freedom to visit other people's homes with ease, or go to a cinema, restaurant or other public building that had steps.

A highlight of every week for me was horseriding. We went to the horseriding centre on a Tuesday afternoon. One of the Shetland ponies had been fitted with a special saddle—the saddle itself was in the shape of a little wicker box, with a low back and sides, and a seatbelt to tie around me. This way I could sit safely and ride independently. I needed the special saddle because if my legs are not straight out in front of me I have no balance at all.

I loved the feeling of being on the horse. My pony was called Arkle—after the famous racehorse. Riding also helped with balance and helped to strengthen my back and leg muscles which were used to stay safely upright when the animal was moving. Arkle was a little eccentric; sometimes we would be walking along calmly when suddenly he would take off with me on his back and go over some of the jumps that had been set out for more experienced riders and bigger horses. I loved when this excitement unfolded but the person leading him and walking alongside me would run screaming after us. Unfortunately Arkle died when I was about 11, and the saddle didn't fit any other horse, so I had to quit riding.

Another highlight was swimming on a Thursday morning. We would be loaded into mini-buses and taken to the pool. There were volunteers there who helped us into our swimming gear, and helped us shower and dress afterwards. The feeling of freedom to move in the water was incredible. Not having arms or legs meant I bobbed along in the water. I learned to do the backstroke, and over a period of time built up the stamina to complete a series of distance badges, right up to the mile badge—I swam a mile up and down the pool. It took me almost three hours to complete and I was exhausted but exhilarated.

At ten or so I got my first powered wheelchair. The sides of my hands were raw all the time from the constant pushing of the old one. My new powered chair didn't fold, so I couldn't take it with me wherever I went and would have to go in a push wheelchair. It was horrible going into a store and not being able to browse without telling someone exactly where I wanted to go, look at, etc. I had no independence and I didn't like it at all. At the time I thought my powered wheelchair was brilliant, but it only went about 4mph. It was only many years later that I acquired an American powered chair that goes really fast, allowing me to go 'jogging' with friends or 'run' with the children.

Every Christmas the school would put on a play. For weeks we would look forward to regular classes being cancelled while we rehearsed for the play. All children, regardless of their ability, would be involved. A stage would be built at one end of the gym/cafeteria with a ramp at the back of it to allow access for the kids in wheelchairs. The plays were varied—one year the *Sugar Plum Fairy* and another year the *Nativity*. So much work must have gone into the production but we loved them and our parents loved to come and watch their kids strutting their stuff on stage. The older kids didn't have to take part directly in the plays, but they had roles such as showing parents where to park, giving directions to the hall, handing out programs or helping with the refreshments afterwards. After the play the parents were invited to tea and sandwiches in the home economics classroom, and the Christmas cakes would be displayed for the parents to see. There was great excitement too backstage (in the classrooms) as we all got into costume and had make-up done, looking out for family and friends in the audience and of course, the fun of learning the lines.

We were also taught how to use computers. These were made available through The Thalidomide Trust. The Trust was designed to be able to supply funds for equipment needed so that people affected by the drug could gain more independence. The Thalidomide Trust supplied word processors (very new back then) to Fleming Fulton school so that those of us who needed them could learn to type and use these machines. They were fairly complicated and we had to learn a series of codes for each letter or word. Eventually almost everyone found it easier just to use the keyboard rather than remember codes and deal with computers that constantly broke down or spewed out the wrong things. The computers back then were large electric typewriters set on a little trolley with a shelf underneath housing a huge computer unit. Each of us, depending on our disability, had a joystick set in a box with 8 little slits. Each slit had a micro switch inside and each switch was numbered 1 through 8. Each letter had a code, for example 'a' would be 7-1. To use the word processor, each word or phrase had a 3 number code, for example 'and' would be 7-1-2. Looking back, they must have expected us to be absolute geniuses to remember a whole book full of codes…so we all learned to type on the keyboard instead.

FAMILY LIFE

MY MOTHER WAS AN ALCOHOLIC AND A WIDOW AND blamed herself for taking the drug which caused my disability. Drinking was her coping mechanism. She drank heavily and she and my oldest sister were always fighting. In fact my oldest sister left home vowing never to come back. She kept her word. Even when she lived at home I felt Phyllis was embarrassed by me; she didn't bring her boyfriends around when I was there. After she had left she even crossed the road one day to avoid me and although, in recent years, I have tried to make contact, she appears to have cut all ties with me.

During the good weather I liked to play outside with the other kids. I didn't like many of them coming into our house in the evening because I was never sure whether my mother would be sober or not. One spring evening, during a Loyalist strike when we had been sent home and the school closed because of long power cuts, my sister Anne went visiting friends with her new

35

husband, Gerry. She gave me the address of the friend they were visiting because she knew that Mom could go off drinking anytime and wanted to be sure I knew where to find her. I was out playing with my friends until dark and went inside at 10pm when everyone else went home. My mother was in the armchair, so drunk she could hardly speak. Then she decided to get up for some reason—and toppled backwards through the front of a china cabinet that was beside and behind the armchair. Glass crashed and she had a huge gash in her arm. I was terrified. We had a large step at the front door and so my wheelchair was still outside. I climbed into my chair and pushed myself next door to the neighbours house. I told them, shamefully, what had happened and told them where my sister was. I can still feel the fear that my mom would die before we got back and the shame that everyone would be talking about us the next day. The neighbours put me in the car and drove me to my sister. She and Gerry followed us home straight away and called for a doctor. By the time we got home my mom had managed to sober up enough to find a towel and wrap it around her arm to stop the blood going everywhere but there was already a huge mess from it. They managed to get her up into bed and began clearing up glass and blood in the living room.

As I mentioned previously, this incident happened during the Loyalist strikes in the early 1970s, so there was a major power cut that night. The doctor came and Gerry had to hold a candle up to allow the doctor to stitch my mother's arm. Never had I wanted to belong to another family as much as I did that night. Now the neighbours knew about her drinking (although they'd probably known long before) and I was ashamed to be part of her family right then.

Later, in my teens, my mom and I discussed her feelings of guilt at having taken the drug but I assured her that the fault lay with the company that had manufactured and distributed the drug. However, I did feel angry. I hated the way people looked differently at me because of my disability. My mom had her problems but over the years she taught me well and there was never any doubt in my mind how much she loved me.

My mom and I were invited to spend a week in a caravan by the sea. She was friendly with a woman called Rosie Johnston and I was best friends with her daughter Elizabeth. When I was home from school we would play together regularly. Elizabeth was number 13 of 17 kids in their family. I loved going to their house because there was always a warm, welcoming feeling with lots of people around.

We had a lovely week in the caravan with the other family but when we came home we got a shock. During the time we were away the house was raided by the British Army in the middle of the night, under the pretence of looking for hidden guns. Of course there were no guns, but the soldiers emptied all the food out of the larder and the fridge onto the floor and trampled it throughout the house into the carpets. They also cut open all my soft toys and pulled the stuffing out, ripped heads off and overturned beds, dressers and anything else they could find. By the time we came home Anne and Gerry had managed to clean up a lot of the mess but I still felt my cuddly toys were dirty now. The Army at the time would regularly do this in Catholic housing estates just to provoke and harass the local population.

Having seen the soldiers in a different light in Belfast beforehand, this incident turned me against them and after that any time they came to the school I would have nothing to do with them. I couldn't understand why someone would want to be so hateful to another person just because of their religion. After all, the soldiers were the ones who shouldn't have been there in the first place.

Trying to Blend in

Some people affected by thalidomide were put through surgeries either to remove parts of limbs so they could fit into prosthetics, or because doctors at the time wanted us to look 'normal'. When I was seven I had surgery to remove a useless little finger that was supposed to allow my other fingers more dexterity but it made little difference as the finger next to the amputated one didn't have a knuckle joint in the first place.

When I was 12 years old the doctors decided that, because my right hand was completely curled up against my arm, I should have surgery to straighten the bone at my wrist. The logic behind the surgery was that if my arm was straighter I would be able to use my fingers on that hand, allowing me to dress easier and also allowing me to hold the steering wheel to drive—when I was old enough. I agreed. I was impatient for independence. Until then I had also needed some help dressing because I only had one functional arm that didn't reach my other side to pull down clothes.

I had my surgery at a hospital in Belfast. Unfortunately, when they broke my arm and pulled it straight, there was not enough skin to stretch and so I was left with an area that took close to six months to heal. I was in a great deal of pain and not able to lift up the middle finger. An X-Ray determined that the pin in my bone was too long and so I had to repeat surgery to have it shortened. My arm was in a cast that had to be changed every two weeks because of the seepage from the unhealed area. I would crack the very top and bottom of the cast while it was still wet—and then slide my arm out to wash it every day and slide it back in again.

Eventually, because my skin was still not expanding to cover the raw area on my wrist, a medication was applied that burned the area closed. Once this was done I didn't need to wear the cast anymore and I was able to start using my fingers. When the pin was removed the bone did bend back in a little, but it is still straight enough to allow me full use of my hand. I then had to learn how to use a hand that had been fairly useless up until that point. I still favoured my left hand for doing things but now I was able to dress myself independently and I hoped to drive my own car some day.

MY MOTHER HAD SET UP A TRUST FOR ME FROM MONIES received from a court case against the manufacturers of the drug. She wanted me to have my own home and a family and put this money in a trust until I was 21. Parents were also given a sum of £10,000 each. Since my father was dead my mother missed out on half of this money, but for the first time we had carpets on all the floors and a black and white television.

When I was 14 I had a best friend at school called Jeanette who had brittle bones. She was the same age as me and we were the oldest kids boarding at that time. We were eventually allowed to go to the local youth club after many arguments about the ludicrously early bedtimes we had to endure and having the person in charge allow us to stay up late enough to go. On a normal night we would be sent to bed at 9pm, but the youth club went on until 10pm so we needed permission to stay up until then.

The club was held at the school on Monday and Thursday evenings. It was called a PHAB club (Physically Handicapped and Able Bodied) and was supposed to be made up of half disabled and half non-disabled kids. We were all aged between 12 and 17 years old. The idea of an integrated youth club at the time was very advanced. Most other youth clubs either had all non-disabled kids or else were held especially for kids with disabilities, with helpers in attendance. At our club the kids all helped each other.

All the teenagers from the housing estate next to the school came to the club and this was a huge deal because we were discovering boys. The highlight of the club was the discos, held four times a year. I was aware that having a disability would never make me Miss Popular with the boys, but I always hoped one of them could see the real me through the disability. Many nights I cried myself to sleep when I saw other girls dancing with guys I liked, knowing they would never want me because I just looked too different. I believed I was ugly and would have to live life alone. I had little self confidence and didn't even know how to approach a boy. I didn't know what way to react if they were fooling around.

At the school there was a member of staff who took delight in being verbally and emotionally cruel to the kids. Everyone tried to avoid her. One day, while my friend and I were talking about boys she told me I needed to face up to some facts of life. She told me that I needed to get used to the fact that people were always going to stare at me because I was different and what boy would ever want to go out with me?

Our youth club was pretty much like any youth club. We had a big hall where the girls would listen to music, chat or practice dancing. There were snooker tables, table tennis, table-top football and an area for board games. Once a month we went to the pool. We took part in regular youth club competitions, competing against all other youth clubs in Belfast at table tennis, snooker, checkers and other games. I became a reasonably good table tennis player and had a bat with an extra long handle so I could reach across the table when playing. We also went on a few adventure weekends and I learnt different sports. We went to a swimming pool and learnt how to paddle kayaks, how to roll in them and how to fall out of one properly and come up beside it. I hated the falling out part because I seemed to always come up inside the overturned kayak. There was an air pocket there and I could breathe but the first couple of times it happened and I didn't surface the instructor almost had a heart attack, thinking I had drowned in his pool. Rolling the kayak was fun but the only way they could stop me spilling out during the roll was to put the cover on the kayak. Otherwise, having no legs I just slid out once I was upside down. In order to compensate for not being able to turn the oar to get the most from the paddle in the water, one oar was set with the ends already turned at a 90° angle to each other which meant I just needed to hold it and be able to move it from side to side in the water.

Once we were proficient we were taken to kayak on Castlewellan Lake in the Mourne Mountains. It was exhilarating but I was terrified that the kayak would roll and I would come up inside it instead of beside it. But I managed to stay afloat and have fun with the other kids there. I not only kayaked on a lake, but also managed to pull myself, with a little help, up the side of a rock wall which was sort of like a small mountain. However, I couldn't absail back down so the rescue stretcher was brought out and I was 'rescued'. That was very funny. I was sat on the stretcher (like a long basket) and a strap was tied securely around my hips and another just under my chest. Then I was lowered over the edge of the wall so I was standing straight up. But then disaster struck—because I had no legs I began to slide down the stretcher and so by the time we reached the ground one strap was up around my neck and I was hanging on for dear life. I think the climbing instructors learned a valuable lesson that day—people need legs to stay in the basket. But it gave all of us a good laugh at the time.

I also learned how to drink alcohol on those weekends; it always made me feel ill the next day. The kids from the housing estate brought along bottles of vodka. After the staff had gone to sleep, we all sneaked back to the living area of the house we were staying at, and the drinking went on 'til the wee hours. I felt part of and accepted by the group.

I was the only Catholic at the youth club because the estate nearby was Protestant. Belfast was divided into ghettos of either Catholic or Protestant and very seldom did kids from both sides meet. I was accepting of them and them of me. I think some of the kids saw me as their mascot because they were very protective of anyone teasing me because of my religion, but of course the kids who were my friends had no problem teasing me and I them.

PEOPLE SEEM TO THINK OF SOMEONE WITH A DISABILITY AS being asexual. I knew boys liked me as a friend but they weren't going to ask me out and this hurt so much. I thought I must be very ugly or plain but this was the hand I was dealt—maybe those people who always said that relationships, marriage, children were not for me were right. But I had a dream that one day, given the chance, I wanted to be a mom, have a husband who loved me and accepted me, and have a home of our own. Mind you, back then I also dreamed of being a movie star, a baker and even marrying Donny Osmond, David Cassidy or one of the Bay City Rollers, who were my idols of the day. The boys at the youth club all went after the most attractive girls. I sat back and watched helplessly—there was no way I could compete.

SCHOOL, TO ME, WAS A PLACE WHERE SOCIAL INTERACTION was the important part of the day. Classes were okay but I had no real desire to learn math, or geography or science. However, luckily for me I had a natural ability for academic subjects and home economics too. Our Home Economics teacher was like a little like Hyacinth Bucket (Bouquet)*. She believed in me and taught me to believe in myself. At the time when we were choosing our O Level subjects the principal of the school told me I should consider more academic subjects because I would not be able to do what was required for the

*A character in the television show *Keeping Up Appearances*.

Home Economics exam. The Home Economics teacher disagreed and I passed O Level Home Economics, having made a full meal (starter, main course and dessert) for an external examiner. I also passed seven other O Levels before I left the school.

Two months before I left school for good, my first car arrived. I had been taken to London for assessment some months prior, and the car (a Ford Escort) was modified so I could drive. The Thalidomide Trust paid for the assessment, the car, the modifications and the driving lessons because there was no accessible public transport in Northern Ireland and in order to be able to get a job or have a quality of life, I needed to be able to move around independently. I was still walking on my little boots, and so the driver side had a little step that dropped down to allow me to climb in. Once on the seat I then pulled a string that was attached to the step and the inside of the car, allowing me to pull up the step which folded neatly at the side of the driver seat. Then I had another string to pull the door closed because my arms were too short to reach out and grab the door. The car was fitted with hand controls and a very crude looking extension was fitted to the handbrake and gear changer to allow me to reach them. The ignition and switches for the lights, wipers and radio on/off were located on the door by my right arm. However, my wheelchair was in the boot and I needed assistance to get it out. But at least this way I didn't need someone with me all the time.

The car was delivered to the school a week or so after my 17th birthday. I was so excited I couldn't concentrate on anything else but the thought of driving. Some of the other older people affected by thalidomide were already driving and now I knew anything was possible for me.

The Thalidomide Trust in England had arranged for a local driving instructor to come to the school to give me lessons in the evening. At my first lesson I didn't even know where the key fitted for the ignition. But we went for a drive around the streets close to the school and then Mr. Leeper, my instructor, astounded me by suggesting on the Friday that I drive to Newry. He said he would drive the car back to Belfast and collect me again on the Sunday.

The trip to Newry was amazing. I had called my mom to tell her I would be driving home. She hadn't believed I had a car, but when she saw me pulling in outside our flat she looked so proud. She called all the neighbors out to see me driving—I was the first in our family to drive. I passed my test a few weeks later, and drove myself home for the summer holidays and the end of my school career.

I finished school with seven O Levels and a few typing exams. Before I left school I had sat the entrance exam for the civil service as a typist and was on a waiting list to be placed in a job in Belfast. But in the meantime I had to stay home and wait.

That summer was memorable. On the 11 July I stayed with friends from the estate. It was an eye opener as on the estate bonfires were lit and people got drunk and spewed spite for the Catholics. Funnily enough I felt safe with my Protestant friends. It made me sad to think that our communities were so divided and there was so much hate. The next day I watched the parades along with my friends' mothers and afterwards four of my friends drove to Newry with me to spend the night. The following morning we went down to Dublin.

Belfast for the most part was divided into religious ghettos, and so these kids had never met Catholics before—except me. When we drove over the border to the south we stopped for petrol and one of the guys who went into the shop was amazed that the people there looked like him, and even spoke the same language.

But the day in Dublin was something else. I noticed as we walked down O'Connell Street that they were all looking behind them. I asked what the problem was and nearly died laughing when they told me their parents had told them to be careful because nuns, sent by the Pope, would grab them from behind and pull them into the Churches and convert them to Catholicism. They also believed the Pope lived secretly in Dublin to make sure the nuns did their job properly.

The summer came to an end and I was still waiting to be placed in my job. Because I had been sent away to school, and we had moved to a more accessible apartment across town from where I had initially grown up, I didn't have many friends in Newry anymore. I saw myself as an outsider, wanting so badly to be able to join in, but not having the self confidence to know how to make friends. The friends I had when I was young were doing their own things, involved in relationships, getting married, having families, and hanging out with the friends they had gone to school with. My school friends were scattered all over Northern Ireland, but none of them lived in Newry.

So I stayed home. I had my car but driving around alone was no fun. I ate junk food and sweets while spending my nights sitting in with my mom, watching television because I had nowhere to go and nobody to hang out with. I didn't want this to be the picture of my life. I wanted more.

In November I was offered a job as a typist in the Civil Service to begin in the new year. I began a strict diet regime and walked as much as I could in my little boots in order to lose some weight.

In January, 1980, I began my first job. Because the job was in Belfast, I secured a place in a 'hostel' for disabled people in Belfast, where I planned to live during the week and come home at weekends. The hostel was a big Victorian house with a couple of bedrooms on the ground level, and more on the upper floors for those people mobile enough to manage the stairs. Most of the people there went to a local day center, where they did menial work for little money. I was the only resident with a job and therefore I was up and gone before everyone else in the morning, and my dinner would be kept in the oven for me when I got home in the evening. I went out most nights—I still had friends from the youth club, and I made other friends over the CB radio.

Once I got my first car I got a CB radio installed. They were illegal in the North but the police tended not to interfere with them so long as people were not giving away their positions so terrorists could take advantage. If there was a bomb scare, the police would use a high pitched blocking sound and if CB users heard this then they stayed off the CB radio. My primary reason for having a CB in the car was in case I broke down so I could contact some of the lorry drivers—who all carried the radios—for help.

One night my friends and I had parked on the New Lodge Road talking to friends on a CB radio (CB radios crossed the religious divide). All of a sudden army vehicles came racing down the road and soldiers jumped out of the back. There was a police officer with them who told everyone to get out of the car. I explained I had a disability and couldn't but everyone else was taken out of the car. Then the police officer sat into the passenger seat and asked me where the CB radio was. There was no point in lying so I showed it to him. I asked was he going to confiscate it, and he told me he wouldn't as long as we moved. Apparently we were sitting at the back of a police station and every time we spoke on the CB we knocked out their radio communications to their vehicles. When the army left we moved quickly, but we laughed about it for weeks later.

MY JOB WAS BORING, BUT AT LEAST I WAS EARNING MONEY and was working like everyone else; living beyond the expectations people had for me. I typed out letters and memos, then they were checked by the supervisor and either sent back for corrections or sent out. Mostly they were sent out. I suspected that my supervisor thought I wasn't promotable but I knew this job wasn't forever. It was a stopgap.

LOVE HURTS

IN AUGUST, 1980, I WENT TO THE US ON A HOLIDAY organized by the Thalidomide Trust. There were 28 of us and 12 helpers. The night before we flew out we all stayed in a hotel in London. I was very shy and quiet because I didn't really know any of the other people there. I was sharing a room for the length of the holiday with a lovely girl who was also thalidomide affected.

I remember flying into JFK airport in New York, feeling the excitement of seeing all the tall buildings and hearing people speak in accents normally reserved for the movies. I didn't have a battery charger that would work in the US because of the differences in voltage so I was in a push wheelchair for the duration of the holiday. Even so, I thoroughly enjoyed the few days we spent in New York. We even took a helicopter trip around the city and the Statue of Liberty. I saw the World Trade Centre as well. Then we went on to Orlando for a week and then Miami for a few days.

I loved Florida—the bright lights, theme parks, the way people spoke, the food, and the sheer size of everything. Disneyworld was the most accessible place for wheelchairs I had been to. It was a revelation—we could go everywhere and even get onto some of the rides. When we were taking off from Miami airport to fly home I knew the US was where I wanted to live and vowed to work towards moving there at some point. The USA was just so far ahead in accessibility for disabled people.

It was strange being on holiday with other disabled people. Since leaving school I had avoided being seen with other people with disabilities because I thought it drew attention to me. I hated being in groups at school as it had felt we were on parade every time we went out as a group. We would all be marched to the park in a group and of course people would look at this single file procession of disabled kids going along the road, being pushed in wheelchairs. The younger kids would sit two to a large wheelchair so it looked even stranger. So I thought if I was the only disabled person in a group I wouldn't draw so much attention to myself. But these other thalidomide people were good to be with. It was, and still is, a strange but somehow comforting experience for me to meet someone who looks a little like me. Almost like a strange type of family. I learnt then that a lot of these people had much more confidence about themselves, their appearance and life in general.

When I came back from the holiday in the US I had a throat infection that kept me from work for another two weeks. When I arrived back to the hostel, things had changed. There were two guys there, both around my age and without disabilities. They were English and had decided to do voluntary work for a year between school and college. One of them was called Colin, and the other Martin. Colin had dark curly hair and was a little strange in that he wanted to be a funeral director or a mortician when he finished college. Martin0—he had blonde hair and was incredibly good looking. He had his sights set on becoming a geologist. I became friendly with Martin over the next few weeks—he would sit with me while I ate in the evenings, come out to the youth club with me and we would talk for hours. At the youth club he was teased about being English, but he always took it in good spirit. He always made the excuse of wanting help doing the crossword in the newspaper in the evening, just so we could spend time together while I was having my dinner. I really liked him but I thought he wouldn't want to go out with someone with a disability.

Then a few weeks before Christmas, he kissed me. I was floating on air. We spent all our spare time together, and though we both had to go home for Christmas, both of us arrived back a day early to be together.

Then the management team at the hostel discovered the relationship and Martin was to be sent home. For our last week together I took time off work and we travelled around. I also wanted to be close to him for as long as possible because I believed that there could not possibly be two guys out there who could want a relationship with me, who could see the real me inside the disability.

The night before he left, he came home to Newry with me and I took him to the train the next morning. I cried all the way back from the train station. I thought that I wouldn't hear from him again. I was inconsolable for weeks, lost interest in living in Belfast and in my job, and decided it might be time for a change in my life. But Martin didn't forget about me—we kept in touch by letter for a long time and he even came to my first wedding.

Around the same time, the hunger strikers in Long Kesh prison began dying. I came back from home after the May bank holiday weekend on a Monday. At 5am the next morning a member of staff came into my room, switched on the light and told me civil war was about to break out and I needed to get out of the city and home as soon as possible. I was on the road by 6am, not knowing what was going to happen or if I would ever even be back. Getting into the car I could hear the constant bang of bin lids in Catholic areas of the city. The roads were almost deserted as people stayed inside waiting to see what would happen. I was petrified not only because of impending riots and unrest but also because a few weeks earlier a young man with a disability had been lifted out of his car and it had been burned and used as a barricade across a road.

Getting out of Belfast was a nightmare. I could only go past the Protestant areas, because there were major riots in the Catholic areas that bordered the motorway. When I was approaching Newry, I was stopped by the police who advised me to turn back. When I told them I lived there they wished me luck and let me through. The town was deserted, except for a group of armed, masked men stopping and hijacking cars on the road. They stopped me and asked where I was going—I told them home and explained where I lived. Fortunately one of them recognized me and they let me through.

For three or four days after Bobby Sands' death we held our breath waiting to see what would happen. But things quieted down and the following week the barricades came down and I went back to work.

One day while I was working in Belfast my mom rang me. She told me that a young soldier had knocked on the door and asked her what the 18ft aerial on the roof was for. She told him that it was attached to my CB radio. Given the illegality of these he was a little surprised and asked if I had a license for it. She explained to me on the phone that she told him 'Now don't be silly. How can she have a license when it's illegal?' The young man was so stunned apparently he just said 'Okay' and walked away. The reason I was crying was because I was laughing so hard. My mom, who was very innocent at times and funny without even realizing it, couldn't understand what was so amusing or why I had to put down the phone on her.

But I still wasn't happy, and now, with taxes, I was earning less than when I started the job, so I quit, went home, and applied to the Technical College to do A levels and word processing classes. I still didn't know exactly what I wanted to do but I knew I could do better than working in a typing pool for the rest of my life.

It had been wonderful to have a guy care for me, even if just for a short time. I now knew what the other girls at the youth club had experienced, but it hurt a lot to lose Martin. As well as having aspirations about a career, I also needed to move on and see if there was a relationship out there for me.

But I still couldn't quite fit in. People still didn't see *me* inside the body of a person with a disability. Would this ever change?

Boldly Going Where Everyone Else Has Gone

I WAS THE FIRST WHEELCHAIR USER TO GO TO THE Technical College in Newry as a student. This caused a huge commotion within the Education Board, who scrambled to ramp one of the entrances and install a disabled toilet for me before the beginning of the term in September. I was glad to be removing barriers for others coming after me.

I was nervous starting college and it was a week before I plucked up the courage to bring my typewriter into class. At break time everyone headed to the cafeteria. I followed along, went up and bought a scone and a glass of milk, and then looked around for somewhere to sit — but all the tables had people at them. I was very shy and didn't want to appear to be barging into someone's conversation by asking to sit at their table. Then a girl came over and asked would I like to sit with them. Her name was Anne. She seemed to know a lot of people, and soon she was introducing everyone to me.

I was driving a Ford Escort Estate car, which allowed me to walk to the back in my little boots, open the boot, and with a type of mechanical arm, lift my chair in and out of the car independently. Although this made me more independent, I still felt that many people could not accept me as their equal. I found I continually had to fight for my rights.

We lived about half a mile from the centre of town, but there were no ramps on the footpaths so getting out of our street was almost impossible. So one Friday I went to see the Roads Service Department at the other side of town. I went in my scooter and explained to the manager that ramps were needed on the footpaths to allow access to town. He looked at me, then patted me on the head and told me to let him worry about it. I was so mad. I went home and wrote a letter to Enoch Powell (MP), telling him what my disability was and asking for help with the problem of the pavements.

Enoch Powell had been the Minister for Health back in the early 1960s and had allowed thalidomide to be distributed through the National Health Service without it being tested properly. He had taken the word of the German company, and the company who licensed it in the UK without properly checking records. Then he refused to see any of the affected children, refused compensation to those affected and did not see the need for a public information campaign on the effects of thalidomide for those who may still have had the pills in their medicine cabinets. I made sure to mention the nature of my disability to him and the fact he was Minister of Health at the time of my birth.

In the meantime I decided to start my own protest by going into town on the busy road, making the lorries and cars go around me and causing traffic chaos in the process. The police stopped me and asked what did I think I was doing, so I told them until there were ramps installed I had no other way of accessing the town I lived in. The police couldn't tell me not to go to the town centre so what could they do but watch helplessly as I disrupted the traffic and pray that I didn't kill myself in the meantime.

The following Saturday morning there was a knock on our front door, which was ajar because my mom was waiting for the groceries she had ordered to be delivered. She yelled out 'Just put them in the kitchen.' Then came another knock, this time on the living room door. She looked up and saw it was Enoch Powell. My poor mom thought of Members of Parliament as next to

God in importance, so she rushed around making him tea and making a fuss of him. I was in the bathroom and oblivious to this until I came out and she confronted me in the hall. 'You don't know your place', she said, 'bringing Enoch Powell here and making him come see you. You're going to get us shot if anyone sees him.'

Mr Powell and I went then went for a stroll into town. I followed my normal protest route and he was clearly shaken at the large trucks whizzing by. He took notes, assuring me that changes would be made quickly, and went on his way.

Monday morning came and the manager of the Roads Service Department rang to ask could he please come to my home to meet me. I agreed. He was impressed that I could summon an MP like that, and so agreed on a program that would begin from our house into town, but would eventually make all of the footpaths in Newry accessible to wheelchair users. The manager kept his word and by the middle of the 1980s Newry was probably the most accessible town for wheelchair users in Northern Ireland.

A few months later another problem arose. I went to the bingo with my sister, only to be told that because there were 3 steps—even though I walked in on my little boots—that I was a fire risk and therefore banned.

So, after a heated argument I left the building, furious and extremely embarrassed. Several other people also left in disgust at how I had been treated. I felt worthless but determined to do something. I went to the papers, and they published a full page spread on the atrocious behaviour of the people in charge of the building, and how they discriminated against people with disabilities. Unfortunately it was the early 1980s and legislation was not in place to stop this type of discrimination.

I LOVED COLLEGE. I LOVED THE CLASSES, THE DISCOS, THE socializing and even managed some studying. I was very shy and not at all confident, but these people seemed to accept me for me, and that was a great confidence booster. But then things would happen that would dishearten me again, like a guy taking a real interest in me at a disco, and then after a while asking could I introduce him to one of the girls who was with us. I realized once again that guys were not seeing me as a woman, but as an asexual person who couldn't possibly be thinking of relationships. I wanted to scream at them that I was as good as them if only they would look beyond my disability.

Even though I knew I would not be involved in a relationship at college, I was also made aware of how accepting my classmates were when exam time came along. Teachers had decided that I should do exams alone in a separate room so that the noise of my typewriter would not disturb the other students. However, my classmates disagreed and finally I was allowed to sit my exams along with everyone else.

But not everyone was as accommodating. One Christmas, while I was still at college I went along to Mass with my sister and her children. As I used a wheelchair, I sat at the side of the pew my family was sitting in. In the middle of the mass, the priest looked down and shouted through the microphone 'Can someone move her, move that cart from the aisle.' I was mortified but refused to move because I wasn't in the way of people going for Communion.

Apparently after the service, several people wrote letters of complaint to the Bishop about the priest's behaviour—once again it was brought home that I was different and even priests would treat me like a second class citizen.

I started working again. My manager was a girl called Deirdre whom I got on very well with and when she went on maternity leave I was asked to step into her role along with another colleague.

Deirdre taught me a lot about being a boss, and a lot about how to treat people well and not expect anything from staff that you're not willing to do yourself. During my time there I also met Cairn. She ran a playgroup for little kids with special needs, a couple of days a week. Cairn was great and we became friends, but then she made a decision to go off to the USA and nanny for a while.

My employment at this particular place was through a government-run employment scheme, and when my year was up I had to leave to make room for the next person on the scheme. Those were tough times in Newry, with unemployment running high and poverty everywhere.

I managed to find a job in a factory in the town— again as an Admin Assistant. However, the manager hired me, I believe, thinking that if they gave me little jobs to do it would take forever and I would feel useful while still not really needing a lot to do. I think it also made him look good that he was employing someone with a disability. But I would be finished my workload by 10am most days—so I left after a while because they didn't really have work for me and I was so bored.

WHY CAN'T YOU SEE I AM
AS GOOD AS EVERYONE ELSE

I FACED MY FIRST EMPLOYMENT DISCRIMINATION WHEN I applied for a job at the local hospital, where I was born. The job description said that I would be working at the front desk in the hospital dealing with the public. I would also carry mail to the wards and do some administrative work. I thought this would be a great job because, unlike many buildings, the hospital was wheelchair accessible and I thought, foolishly, that people would be more understanding and accepting of my disability.

So armed with the fresh-faced confidence of youth I went for my interview. I knew the hospital was accessible so that was the major obstacle overcome. However, I was shocked during the interview when the interviewer told me straight up that someone like me wouldn't portray a good image of the hospital to the public. Then she asked me how I would carry the mail to the wards. I told her my hands worked perfectly well and that would not be a problem for me. I also told her that I was very disappointed that the hospital where I had been born did not think it a fitting thing for people to see me.

When I got home I called the Ombudsman's office but I was told that, at that time, there was no discrimination legislation covering people with disabilities. I was so angry that people with disabilities in general were thought so little of that they were not even protected by laws that protected the rights of many other minority groups. That was the point in my life I decided I needed to be working on civil rights for people with disabilities.

Even though unemployment in Northern Ireland was high, and even though other people with disabilities I knew said they could never find a job, I always managed to find work, and was rarely without something to do. When I wasn't working for money, I volunteered at a local day centre, working with people who suffered with mental illness.

It was during my time volunteering at the centre that I met a guy I had grown up with. When we were kids he had stared at me and asked silly questions about my disability so I told him I was really a witch and could turn him into a frog anytime I wanted. After that any time he saw me he had run screaming in the opposite direction. At the time I had thought nothing more of it, but apparently I had scared him so badly that he still remembered it and still wasn't a hundred per cent sure that it wasn't the truth.

After volunteering for a couple of months I decided it was time to go back to college again to gain a Certificate in Business Studies and spent a wonderful two years taking courses for the Certificate in Newry Technical College. By this time, of course, the Tech was accessible for wheelchair users and my confidence had grown a little so it was a much better experience for me.

When I was 21 I had my first experience of having my heart broken because of my disability. Silly as it may sound, up until then I always thought deep down that if someone didn't like me, or preferred another girl, it was because I wasn't good looking, or not trendy in my dress sense, something like that. I thought that if someone had a problem with my disability they wouldn't show such an interest in me. But I was talking on the CB radio one night when I got talking to John. He lived in a town nearby, and over the next week or so we talked almost every night. He seemed really interested in me and so one night, after he said he wanted to meet me,

I told him about my disability. He said it didn't matter and he still wanted to meet me.

For the next few weeks, John would come to our house and we would go for a drive or just sit talking in the car. Even though we never got as far as a relationship I really believed we were going in that direction from things he said. I was smitten and began to let my guard down and believe that maybe there was someone for me after all. Then one night he told me he couldn't see me anymore. When I asked why, he said 'What would I do if any of my friends saw me with you?' I was shattered. It was only then I saw myself as others did. I was devastated and felt like a freak. I was convinced that I would never meet anyone and would spend my life alone. I know that we hadn't really become 'an item' but believed our relationship was definitely heading that way.

Over the next few days I sank lower than I had ever felt, and I even contemplated suicide. I stopped taking care of my appearance or going out, thinking there was no point in living if my life was to be that of a freak to be stared at, pointed at and devoid of ever experiencing a relationship. It was the only time in my life I felt really angry at being born with a disability that made me stand out.

But gradually, with the help of friends, I began to pick myself up again. I didn't have any confidence in myself, though. Shortly after this experience a friend sent me a copy of an Irish newspaper. On the page was a picture of a thalidomide affected Irish woman called Maggie who was trying to get in touch with other thalidomide people. I called the number on the page, and arranged to meet Maggie the following Sunday, in Dublin where she lived. I persuaded my friend Anne to come along, so that if Maggie turned out to be strange or awful, she could make the excuse of meeting her boyfriend that evening so we could get away fast.

Maggie was about 3ft 8 inches with arms shorter than mine, and an air of self-confidence that was awesome. She was from Donegal but lived in Dublin and went to college there. She walked around the city wearing headphones and listening to a stereo, while looking like she didn't care what other people thought. We got on great. This was the start of a lasting, fun-filled friendship.

Over the next few years Maggie and I would meet up at weekends in Dublin. I would stay in her bed-sit with her. I left a camp bed there and would drive down on a Friday evening after work. Then we would get ourselves changed and ready for our night out, order a taxi and go to the Phoenix Park racecourse where there were three bars and a nightclub under the stands of the racecourse. The wheelchair I had at the time came apart and so we would have the taxi driver take it apart and put it in the boot and set it up at the other end under the watchful eye of Maggie.

The first night we did this we went into the nightclub and sat down with our drinks. The music was playing and a group of maybe eight guys were all dancing in a circle. At first I thought we had wandered into a gay disco. So, when this good looking blonde guy from the group walked past to go to the toilets, I asked him was he gay or did all guys in Dublin dance together? He laughed and asked what if they were? I told him we all have our problems, but deep down I was thinking 'what a waste for womankind'. When he came back from the toilets he was still laughing and lifted my drink, asking would I like to join them. We all joined them and they turned out to be a great bunch of people.

The guy's name was Ciaron, and we became firm friends. Some weekends I would stay at his house when I came to Dublin, and I became friends with all his family. Ciaron always accepted me for who I was, and over time I realized he was as unsure of himself as I was about me. I realized that this was part of growing up and nothing to do with my disability. Although we were never officially in a relationship, the closeness we shared—as well as a few snogging sessions—meant that I began to see myself in a different light, and began to believe that maybe there was someone out there for me who could see through my disability and would be prepared to love the real me. I began to believe that maybe I wasn't so ugly.

On the weekends that Maggie was busy, or off visiting family or friends, I would stay with Ciaron and I would sometimes go grocery shopping with his mom on a Saturday while he was working with his dad—a plumber. Ciaron's mom was warm and funny. She never thought twice about him having a friend with a disability and I was accepted almost as part of the family.

After about a year or so, Ciaron and some of his friends all went out to Australia for a year. However, Ciaron loved it there and decided to become an Australian citizen and stay. As far as I know he's still there, married to an Australian girl.

Mom

In 1985, after years of coughing from smoking, my mom was sent into the hospital for tests on her lungs. She was there for a week and at the end of her stay my sister and I were told that she had terminal lung cancer. One lung was completely destroyed and the other was not far behind. My mother was of the generation that never questioned doctors, and so the doctor agreed that he would not volunteer the information to my mother but if she asked for her diagnosis he would tell her.

We told her she had bronchitis from smoking for such a long time. She accepted this and was walking around, in little pain, for almost another 2 years. During this time of course the first thing we did was panic, thinking that she was going to die immediately. I gave up work so that she wouldn't be alone during the day and my sister Anne would walk from her house to ours almost every day, bringing her children to see their Granny.

Leigh Gath

For her birthday, Anne and I decided to take our mom to a nice restaurant for a meal. She didn't eat out much so this was a big treat. While we were in the restaurant, mom went to the bathroom. She was gone quite a while so just as my sister was getting up to look for her, she came back looking a little flustered. She announced that she didn't like those bathrooms because there was only one toilet stall and there were these weird looking little sinks near regular looking sinks. She couldn't understand why we were laughing so hard we could hardly sit up. She had accidentally used the men's toilets.

Toward the end of her life, my mother suffered what looked like a stroke one day. She was sitting in the armchair when I left to take my niece home, but when I came back 20 minutes later she had fallen over to the left and was gasping for breath. I called an ambulance and when they arrived explained to them that she didn't know she had terminal cancer. I gave them the medication she was taking to help her breathe and they passed the information and medication on to the hospital. I raced to Anne's house and we both followed the ambulance to the hospital. Of course, the doctors in the hospital believed that because she had cancer she must be in pain and gave her powerful pain killers.

That happened at the beginning of December 1986, and we spent as much time as possible at the hospital with her. By Christmas Eve she was walking with a walking frame and doing well. She had always been a heavy woman but in the previous couple of months the weight had fallen off her so we believed the end was near. She, however, thought that it was because she had been successfully dieting.

Mom came home for Christmas and we invited her best friend around for dinner. We had a lovely family day and she went to bed happy that night. But she had lost so much weight over the previous month or two we knew this would be her last Christmas.

Since she had come home from the hospital I left both bedroom doors open at night so that I could hear if she needed me. The next morning I was woken by my mom calling me. She told me she couldn't get out of the bed and felt she needed to go back to the hospital. So I called an ambulance and then called my sister to tell her to meet us there.

My mom was in hospital for a further three weeks, all the time becoming weaker. We took turns staying with her—I would stay during the day and Anne would come when the kids were at school. Gerry,

Anne's husband, would spend the nights at the hospital with Mom. Over the years they'd had their run-ins but now it was Gerry that she wanted to stay with her at night. By now she knew that she was dying but it was something that was never mentioned.

The weather was terrible around Christmas and New Year that year. There was very heavy snow and it was impossible for me to get my car out. So one night when Gerry called to say mom was looking very weak, I called the local police station and explained my situation. They sent out an armoured car, lifted me and my chair up into the back and drove me to the hospital. They told me to call when I needed a lift back home. Considering that they were putting themselves at risk by driving into Newry, I thought that was an amazing gesture. It was like a mini miracle when she woke up and was reasonably chatty and bright.

Early one morning about a week later I got a call from Gerry again at the hospital. He had spent the night with Mom, and he told us to come quickly. I dashed to the hospital and a few minutes later my mom died peacefully.

I drove to a quiet spot and cried. I had never seen anyone die before. Even though I had my own apartment now, I had spent so many nights with my mother at her place that now there was a big hole left.

We passed the word to my oldest sister that our mother had died but she didn't come to the wake or funeral. However, Ciaron's family hired a mini-bus and came from Dublin for the funeral.

When the funeral was over we began the job of clearing out my mother's apartment. It belonged to the Housing Executive and they would eventually want it back to rent to someone else. We gave her clothes to charity and the television to the Hospice. We took a few mementoes for ourselves but for the most part her things went to help others. Leaving her flat for the last time was very hard. It had been my home for 10 years and even though my own place was in a different town it would always be strange to drive past, knowing she wasn't there anymore.

I had bought my own apartment in Warrenpoint the previous year. I became terrified of being alone in the dark of night, which I discovered later was part of the grieving process. So I took to sitting up all night reading or watching movies, only feeling safe enough to sleep once it got to about 5.30am and I knew the milkman would be around soon. This went on for months and I could only sleep when someone else was staying over.

DISABILITY ACTIVISM

WHEN MY MOTHER DIED I KNEW I NEEDED TO GET back to work. Around that time an organization called Disability Action was setting up a satellite office in Newry to work with people with disabilities and their families who lived in South Down and South Armagh. They were looking for someone to run the office. I applied and was successful. A woman named Margaret was the part-time Admin person for the office and I became the Development Officer. We were based in what had been a little gatehouse at the entrance to what had been an estate, but was now converted into offices for Social Services.

We had one office with two desks in it, and the office at the other end of the building was used by social workers. We all shared the little kitchen area and bathroom.

It was our job to make sure that people with disabilities in the area knew about us, had help applying for benefits and had access to driving assessments through our organization. We also did some work on behalf of people concerning access issues in the area.

One night I was at a late meeting in Crossmaglen and was driving home at around 11pm. Suddenly I saw a red torch waving up ahead on the dark country road. I knew that it couldn't be the British army because the area was far too dangerous for them to be on the road. They even had to take their trash out by helicopter from their army base.

I stopped at the check point and was confronted by several guys wearing ski masks and carrying large guns. I opened the window and one of them asked for my license. I was terrified that they were Protestant paramilitary because if they were, and they saw a Catholic name on my license, then I was as good as dead. One of the men took the license and looked at it. I waited for the shot that would kill me and imagined someone finding my body the next day. Then the man asked me about some relatives, asking did I know them. Once it was established who I was, he told me to go on. He said my car would be watched coming and going from the village and I had nothing to fear driving out there. He also told me several people in Crossmaglen had been really happy with the service offered to them by Disability Action and keep up the good work. It was a totally surreal conversation and I was still shaking by the time I got home.

HE LOVES ME

AFTER MY MOM DIED I FELT THE NEED TO GET AWAY. So that summer, 1987, my friend Maggie and I decided to go on holiday to the Thalidomide Trust hotel in Jersey in the Channel Islands. We knew the hotel would be accessible and we'd meet other people and have a laugh. We had already been on holiday in Ireland and been to the Isle of Man together so we knew we could physically manage.

We got a ferry to Wales and drove through Wales and England to Portsmouth where we got onto an overnight car ferry to Jersey in the Channel Islands. On the ferry we met other thalidomide people who were headed to the same hotel as ourselves.

Arriving in St Helier, Jersey we followed directions to the hotel. Driving in I saw someone peering out through the kitchen window, but didn't realize I had just laid eyes on my future husband.

Like any other woman in her 20s, I dreamt of meeting a good looking guy who could see through my disability and fall in love with me. That was just a dream—in reality people who looked like me never got the good looking man. Or else the man would be stolen away by some good looking girl who didn't have a disability, or would just go out with you because you had something they wanted to con you out of. Well, that's what I thought before I met the man who was not only to love me, but marry me.

When we arrived at the hotel the manager was very excited and insisted we meet the chef, Declan, who was also Irish. I expected some big, fat, baldy man to come out of the kitchen, but instead this good looking young guy with red hair and the greenest eyes shyly came out and said hello before scurrying back to his kitchen.

The next night Maggie and I went out with a crowd of other people to a nearby pub. During the evening Declan arrived and came to sit with everyone. By the end of the night he was sitting beside me, but he was very quiet and so I decided to take on the challenge of having him talk to me properly before the holiday was over. We arrived back at the hotel from the pub, and as it was only 10.30pm we didn't want to go to bed. I'd had a couple of drinks and couldn't drive, so I looked around for someone who could drive my car. Then I saw Declan watching the news and I asked him could he drive. He said yes and I threw him my keys and asked him to take us to a nightclub in town.

Maggie, Declan, a guy called Alan, and myself all set out to town. While Maggie and Alan danced, Declan and I talked—about Ireland, a little about ourselves, our families and all sorts of other things. While we were talking he told me he had been in Jersey working the previous year with his girlfriend from Dublin. She was not on the island this time, but he made it sound like they were still together. I really was getting to like this guy but I reckoned I didn't stand a chance and so why make a fool of myself? We got back to the hotel and he said goodnight and went off to bed. That seemed fairly obvious to me that he was only driving us, and wasn't interested in me at all.

The following afternoon we were sitting sunbathing by the pool at the hotel when Declan came out to sunbathe during his time off. Again we got chatting and this time he told me that he was not seeing anyone either on the island or back in Ireland, but that he had been working on getting a visa to go to work in

Thailand for a year. His visa had arrived and he was leaving for Thailand at the beginning of November when his contract finished in Jersey.

In Jersey there was a strange law that allowed discos to open on a Sunday night, but unless it was a private club, nobody was allowed to dance. If you got up to dance the bouncers would ask you to leave. Declan knew some people at the flying club, and so he asked Maggie and myself if we'd like to go. We both agreed, but about an hour before we were to leave, Maggie announced she wouldn't be going. She knew I liked Declan and had decided that she was going to spend the evening with some other people from the hotel who we had become friendly with. I was sure when I told Declan that he would call it off, but instead he asked would I still like to go with him. I was so nervous. I wasn't sure if anything would happen between us. I was scared in case he kissed me and I turned out to be a horrible kisser.

We had a wonderful time together, meeting friends of Declan's. We even met an American called Fred who had gone to a rugby game in England, met the squad and had taken them up on their invitation to come to the Channel Islands with them for a party. He was a lot of fun, and unknown to us then, would become our best man a few years down the road. Afterwards we went to a little car park by a beach and just talked for a long time, with both seats pushed back and me lying in Declan's arms. Eventually we both fell asleep, and when we woke it was getting bright. Panicking, we drove back and I sneaked back to my room while Declan went to make a start on breakfasts. Of course people had heard the car drive up at 6am and we got a terrible teasing about it.

Over the course of the next two weeks, we spent all our spare time together. We went out for a meal, went to discos, we went for walks. One night we were in a nightclub and Declan was lifting me up steps where a group of us were all sitting, when I whispered 'I love you' in his ear. He just stopped and looked at me. I thought I had blown it and he'd be off like a shot, but instead, after the disco, he told me he felt the same but was scared because his last girlfriend had betrayed him. He also told me our timing for meeting was really bad because he was supposed to go to Thailand for a year. We began holding hands—it was such an incredible feeling to have a man who wanted to publicly hold my hand as we strolled along, and to tell me I was beautiful. I was floating on air. The first time Declan kissed me my heart raced, hoping I wouldn't mess it up. But it all felt so right and so natural.

The day that we were leaving for home Declan was able to take the day off and we went into town. He bought me a beautiful bracelet, and although he had another 8 weeks to work on his contract, we agreed to talk on the phone regularly and we decided to meet in London at the end of October. I would drive over and he would fly in from Jersey, then we would spend five days together in London, and if we still felt the same about each other we would go back to Ireland and he would forget about going to Thailand, otherwise we would part and go our separate ways.

I was sad to leave Declan, really believing this could just be a holiday romance. But I was no sooner home than a bouquet of flowers arrived from him, and we talked on the phone almost every night. He sent me at least two love letters a week. He would quote poems or the words of romantic songs. He seemed to be as much in love as me. Once he even called and told me from a phone box when there was a hurricane blowing and he wanted to get back to the hotel in case he was blown over the sea wall. He was calling from a pay phone up the coast road from the hotel. Later I found out the telephone box he had called from was, minutes later, ripped from the ground and blown into the sea. Damage in the Channel Islands was terrible but fortunately Declan was not hurt, although he had to go the whole way back to the hotel on his hunkers using the low sea wall for protection in case he was blown into the sea.

People at home were skeptical about whether this was more than a holiday romance. Friends of mine told me these things didn't normally happen and to be careful, especially as we had decided to move in together when Declan came back to Ireland. Friends who felt they had my best interests at heart told me to watch that he wasn't just using me. After all, working in the Thalidomide Trust-run hotel he would have been aware we all had a small amount of compensation, as well as government benefits.

When he told his mom about me and my disability she just told him to be careful what he was getting into. Never having met me she thought I needed a carer and was afraid that was going to be his role. When we met and his parents got to know me they realized that I was very capable and very much in love with their son and so I was accepted and treated as part of the family.

Eight weeks later I was in London. I drove over a couple of days early and stayed with my friend Veronica. I was very nervous but I was at the airport on time to pick Declan up. His flight was three hours late because of fog, and when he walked, or should I say staggered, through the arrivals hall, he told me it was because all flights were delayed from Jersey and so all the staff who were flying to different locations, got together in the bar and things got a little out of hand. Of course I believed this man I loved. I didn't want to believe I had gotten together with someone who had a drink problem. My fears seemed groundless as we spent the next few days in London. He was attentive, didn't drink and we had a wonderful time together.

On the way home, we missed the early afternoon ferry because we had got stuck behind a slow moving tractor, and so we had to wait around in Holyhead and get the late ferry, arriving in Dublin early morning. We would go sleep for a few hours at Declan's parents' house, stay the night with them and meet some of his friends, then go back up to the North where we would be living together.

The second clue that he may have had a drink problem happened on the boat. I fell asleep and Declan stayed up, apparently in the bar playing cards and drinking for the three-hour crossing. We were no sooner into the car but he passed out, and I had to pull over and spend time yelling at him and shaking him to bring him around enough to be able to show me where his parents lived. But I put this down to tiredness because it was only much later did he tell me he was drinking all night.

Declan had applied for jobs in Warrenpoint—the town where I lived, before he came back to Ireland and at the interview the following day got the job as chef in a busy restaurant/bar in the town.

It took a while for Declan to get used to living with someone with a disability like mine. In the beginning he wanted to do everything for me because it was easier for him than me. I had to sit him down and try to make him understand that although I loved him spoiling me, it was very important that I keep doing things to maintain the independence I had worked so hard to achieve. One day he walked into the kitchen while I was cooking sausages for our dinner. I was frying by holding a flat spatula in my teeth and turning the sausages with it. My face was very close to the pan but I have never been burned by grease because I dry fry everything. He took one look and told me he would be in the living room. He couldn't bear to watch in case I got burned.

When I met Declan I couldn't cook and really I didn't see the need to cook for one when I could eat frozen meals, or eat at my mother's house or later on after she died, at my sister's house. The first day he arrived at our apartment he opened the freezer and it was stacked high with Bird's Eye frozen meals—mainly spaghetti bolognaise. Being a chef he laughed and after packing everything up to give to friends he set about teaching me to cook.

Christmas 1987 was our first together. Declan had to work but we got up early and opened our presents, and then drank a glass of champagne and orange juice before he had to leave. While he worked all day I visited family, knowing that all our Christmases from now on would probably be like this. He brought home two plated dinners that evening, and we enjoyed our first Christmas dinner in front of the fire, watching TV.

The first two years we were together were fine. Declan was so romantic—he would bring home a little bar of chocolate at night from work, or buy me a book he knew I was looking for, or cook special dinners for us. We went out one night a week to eat and have a couple of social drinks with friends. Declan worked late at the weekends so our time together was on weekdays. But then I began to see cracks coming in our relationship. One Saturday morning we had a row and he packed his bags and left. I was worried silly and decided to go to Dublin to his mom's house to see was he there. She said he had been and told me which friend he had gone to see. I followed him and he said he needed a night's break. I was so worried but I went home anyway. Next morning he called me to go to Dublin to get him, but I was still mad at him and told him he got himself there, so he could get himself home again.

For my birthday in 1989, Declan told me he had a surprise for me but it was far away. He had me get in the car and drive while he gave directions at each town which way to go next. We drove right across Ireland to Carrick-on-Shannon, where he said we needed to stop for lunch. At the hotel he went and made a phone call, and when we finished lunch we went down to the docks where a little motor cruiser was waiting for us. Declan had arranged with my boss for me to have the week off, and had packed a suitcase and loaded it into the boot when I wasn't around. We spent four wonderful days on the cruiser, stopping off at various little towns for lunch or for dinner, and tying up where we wanted for the night. On our last night we bumped into a crowd of people from Newry that we knew and spent a great evening on their boat singing, laughing and reminiscing. That was probably the most romantic thing he ever did for me, and I was blissfully happy then, certain we would be together forever.

In 1990 we bought a house in Warrenpoint, and Declan spent his days off work painting the rooms. He had changed jobs by this time—I thought it was because of better hours and more money, but I found out later on that he had been fired for turning up drunk after his split shifts in the afternoon. As chefs at that time were in short supply, he got another job within a couple of days without me knowing about it. I only found out through his former employer when he lost the second job that he had lost both jobs through turning up drunk for his shifts once too often. The fact that everyone else in Warrenpoint seemed to know about this before me really hurt and I was so embarrassed it was hard to hold my head high.

He had proposed on Christmas Day 1989, and we were busy getting ready and making plans for our wedding, to be held in August 1991. Looking back, the changes had already begun to creep in, but it all began to unravel Christmas 1990. We had a New Year's Eve party with several friends at our house. Declan was working New Year's Day and he went off to bed around 1am. By this time there were two friends left, and we were chatting away when Neil asked me did I know that every night when Declan left work he would go to a bar and instead of having one pint of Guinness as he told me, he would have three pints and three large gins. Neil was amazed we could afford that, after buying the house. He was also amazed that I was okay with Declan driving my car home a lot of nights in this inebriated state.

I kept a closer watch on the bank account, and realized Declan was not putting his share for bills into the account. However, having no self confidence I was afraid he would walk away from me, and I could not have handled that. I was convinced at that time that if he didn't marry me, then who else would ever want me. But I also began watching him when he came home at night, and I began making more excuses as to why I needed the car in the evenings, so he needed to taxi home.

In 1990, one morning we were leaving our apartment for work when the phone rang. I rushed back to answer it but it was a wrong number. As we drove along the seafront toward the main street of Warrenpoint, there was a tremendous bang that shook everything, including the car. The echo of the bang reverberated down Carlingford Lough. Instinctively we knew it was a bomb. As we turned the corner off the seafront we could see a plume of black smoke hanging over the police station.

As we drove down the street towards it, the sight is etched in my brain of a shopkeeper standing outside his shop in shock, lifting large pieces of his shop window and trying to put them back in place. He had a dazed look on his face and blood running down his head. Other people had blood on them like they had been hit with flying glass and shrapnel. Five houses that stood beside the police station were just rubble now, and there was a terrifying silence all around. Someone yelled to us to go to Newry and get help because the phone lines were damaged. In shock we drove to Newry (about five minutes away) and called the police and ambulance services from my office. It turned out one person was killed and many more injured. There had been no warning. It had been left in an alley between a hardware store and the police station, but because of the extra concrete walls of the police station to protect against attack, the blast had gone the other way and destroyed the hardware store and the adjoining houses. The victim of the bomb was young girl working in the store—she was decapitated by the blast. Luckily most people in the houses had either left for work or school when the blast happened, but there was at least one woman, who had been in the shower at the time, seriously injured. The cistern from the old fashioned toilet had flown off the wall and hit her in the face.

Shortly after the bomb attack we began looking for a house. Declan had proposed on Christmas morning, 1989, and we had set a date in August 1991. We found new bungalows being built about a mile from town and the builder agreed to modify the bungalow to suit my needs. We had someone fix up the garden and plant grass as well.

I loved our new house but knew we would not be there forever. I could never see myself raising a family there. The bungalow was on a hill overlooking Warrenpoint, with spectacular views of Carlingford Lough stretching out below. If there was ever another attack on Warrenpoint, the house was high enough and far enough away not to be affected but close enough to walk into town on a summer's day or in the evening to go for a drink. It had three bedrooms and a nice garden, but the garden was on a steep slope so I felt that this was not a place to bring up children, should we be blessed with them.

Having little self esteem I could not deal with his alcoholism. I knew that Declan had a drink problem but I wanted to blank out the potential problems ahead. The week before we married, Declan went to Dublin airport to collect a friend of ours coming from the USA. The airport was only about an hour from our house, maybe an extra 30 minutes allowing for traffic. We didn't have mobiles back then so I had no way of keeping in contact with him. He left about 4pm and should have been back by 8pm. I had dinner made for both of them. Six hours later he arrived back, obviously with drink taken. Our friend, Fred, was fairly shaken up and explained to me that after collecting him, Declan insisted on going to meet his parents in a pub where he downed three or four pints before driving back to our house. Fred wouldn't have gotten in the car with him except that he didn't know anyone else in Ireland. Declan's excuse for the tardiness was that the flight had been delayed.

Really I should have known then that trouble was down the line.

If I Don't Marry Now, I May Never Have the Chance

WE MARRIED IN AUGUST, 1991, BUT I HAD A LITTLE voice in my head telling me that this was not the way to go. I thought this was my only chance at happiness — and so what if he was drinking. Didn't everyone in Ireland drink? Weren't there many happy marriages? And sure didn't he love me!

A few days before the wedding we had our hen and stag nights. Again the alarm bells should have been ringing wildly when Declan had passed out by 10pm and his friends put him to bed at the local hotel. We stayed out until about 1am and then continued the party at our house, just having a good time, singing along with the person who had brought a guitar.

On the Eve of our wedding Declan stayed at the local hotel with the best man. I had warned the best man, his friend Terry, not to let him drink the day of the wedding. Even then I knew I shouldn't be having visions of Declan staggering up to the altar but I loved him and it was too late to go back on plans now. We met all the friends and relatives for one drink after the rehearsal before we went our separate ways.

I walked up the aisle in my little boots to the singing of *The Wedding Song* from Godspell and we sat on chairs before the priest for the ceremony. My friend Maire had organized for her daughter to sing and her nephew to play the guitar. At the communion *Wind Beneath My Wings* was sung and there was hardly a dry eye in the house.

The ceremony and the reception went off perfectly. Declan got down on his knees and we danced our first dance together with me in my little boots. We stayed at the hotel that night and the next morning set off on our honeymoon to California and Hawaii.

We had a great time travelling California, Nevada and Hawaii. In California I learned that the word 'craic' means something different there. We checked into our hotel in San Diego and I went down to reception and asked the receptionist was there somewhere we could eat close by, somewhere with a bit of 'craic' (pronounced crack). He looked horrified and told me he wouldn't know. I thought it a bit strange that he worked there but didn't know the area. It was only when Declan joined me that I realised what I had said—so after some explaining to the receptionist he saw the funny side and directed us to a nearby restaurant.

After being in San Diego for a couple of days we decided to drive to Las Vegas and stay one night there so that we could get a real feel for the place. The drive through the Mojabi Desert was incredible. Miles of nothing except sand and cactus plants growing here and there. It was so hot that signs were posted telling people to turn off their air conditioning in case their cars overheated. At one point we rounded a bend and saw below us the golden arches of McDonald's.

About an hour later we reached Las Vegas, but seeing the lights of the strip on television is nothing compared to the real thing. After checking into our hotel, we went into our first casino and played the poker machines. I put in $1 but got $50 back in coins. Rather than change them back, we decided to walk along the strip to the next casino. As we walked along, with me carrying the cup of money on my lap, people walking the opposite direction kept throwing coins in. At first I didn't know what they were doing until I saw a man with one leg sitting on the sidewalk begging. He was giving me filthy looks. I began to laugh. People passing us thought I was begging and I was, in turn, stealing his business.

Later that night we were walking hand in hand down the strip in Las Vegas towards our hotel when Declan began talking of the future and us going back there for our 10th wedding anniversary I felt cold shivers down my spine, and as hard as I tried I could not picture us together then.

A friend of mine had designed a voltage convertor for my charger so that I would be able to bring my power chair on honeymoon with me. Travelling in the US with my powered chair made me aware of the vast difference in access for wheelchair users. In America it was so easy and accessible.

We went to Hawaii for the final week of our honeymoon. While there one evening we went into a local bar/restaurant for dinner. We met a man called Gil who was there with some work mates. By the end of the evening Gil had invited us to see his job—he worked in the aircraft control tower at the airport on the island. It was a fascinating place to visit and we got to see people bring aircraft in for landing and others see aircraft off the island. We also went to see him in his apartment before we left the island and meet his macaw who went around the apartment on his shoulder. What made the holiday even better was the fact the travel agent in Newry had booked us into the Hilton Holiday

Resort but the tower she had booked us into was not wheelchair accessible and so when we arrived we were transferred to a much smaller building, with its own pool on the roof and concierge service for the guests. Of course, because the mistake was not ours, we got all this luxury for the same price even though in reality it cost a whole lot more. The building was right on the beach and there were lots of accessible walkways around —even one through the sand down to the water's edge. We enjoyed sunset walks, dinner overlooking the ocean and it all made our honeymoon even more romantic. When we would use the hotel pool, Declan would lift me in and then hold me as we splashed, swam and played in the pool. I felt so safe then.

The honeymoon went so well and we were so close that I began to think that maybe, now we were married, things would settle down and Declan would not feel the need to be drinking as much. I arrived back at LAX airport in California looking forward to beginning our married life together.

Sometimes Love isn't Enough

During our return flight with Virgin airlines, Richard Branson was aboard and presented us with a lovely bottle of champagne in a presentation box as he asked us if we were flying for business or pleasure and we told him we were coming home from our honeymoon. On our way over to the USA, the airline had sent us off the flight with a load of alcohol miniatures as a little wedding gift. They also gave us several little bottles of champagne. Declan was great during the honeymoon and drinking was not an issue at all, or at least I thought at the time that it wasn't. I asked him where all the little miniature drink bottles that the Virgin airline staff had given us on our way to the US had gone. Turns out on the nights I was asleep in our room during the honeymoon he would sit up drinking them until he passed out.

Shortly after we returned Declan came home from work one night complaining of feeling unwell and having a bad headache. During the night his temperature went sky-high and in the morning he was so covered in spots he looked like the creature from the black lagoon. He had the chicken pox. The doctor prescribed medication but for days Declan looked and felt terrible. I thought it was a good thing that he couldn't go out because maybe, with the alcohol out of his system he would stay sober now. But one day when he strolled into town for the newspaper I was looking for a document and I opened the drinks cabinet. We had always had a few strange looking bottles of liqueur there and he had never touched them because he didn't like the taste. But all of the bottles were now empty. In the space of four days or so he had managed to drink every drop of alcohol in the house. Although I was concerned, I felt so alone because I couldn't tell anyone. I felt if I did I would be betraying my husband and somehow people would look at me with pity or that 'I told you so' look. I asked him about it and he quite openly told me he was an alcoholic and needed the alcohol to be able to function properly.

At the time I was attending college to get a diploma in Business studies. That December, on the night of Declan's work Christmas party I had an exam. He told me he was disappointed that I couldn't go, but he would go for the meal, then I was to call him at a certain time and he would come home because he would rather spend the night with me. I came home from the exam, poured myself a glass of wine and called him. He said he would be home shortly and I settled down to watch TV. About half an hour later he came in and I saw his threatening side for the first time. He began screaming at me that he could never enjoy a night out without me nagging him to come home. He then lifted the bottle of wine (still full except for the glass) and hurled it against the wall where it smashed. Then he lifted the glass and did the same, smashing it into a thousand little pieces. I was frightened so I went outside, jumped in the car and pulled around the side of the house so he would think I'd gone if he came looking. I stayed there for about half an hour in the cold, before going back inside. He was in the living room—he had cleaned up most of the glass but had cut his hand in the process and was bleeding heavily. He bandaged it and I went to bed—locking the bedroom door behind me. Next morning he was up before me; I could hear him moving around. When I came out he apologized and begged me not to throw him out. He had scrubbed all the marks out of the carpet, but he'd hit the wall so hard with the bottle he had knocked a hole into the wall that would need plastered and painted. We had to have someone come and clean the carpets properly for us, as well as repair and repaint the part of the wall that had been damaged.

For the rest of that year things went from bad to worse. He was openly drinking heavily now, and lost his job in the Aylesforte House. He went to work in a little restaurant in the main Square called Diamonds —a family run restaurant. The owner of Diamonds 'let it slip' the first couple of times Declan showed up hungover, late, or went missing for an hour.

I went on a training course to the Netherlands for a month in 1992. Declan was attending AA meetings that he had started going to before I left. At the end of the course he flew over to meet me and we spent five days together travelling around the Netherlands. Everything seemed fine then except I knew he had been drinking the night he arrived, but he'd acted reasonably sober so I let it go.

Returning home I discovered that Declan had taken £400 out of the account. He admitted to taking the money after I confronted him but said he was back at his AA meetings and it wouldn't happen again.

The owner of Diamonds was very good to Declan, but the day Declan left for a late lunch and never went back, he was let go. That evening as I was driving home from work he lurched out of a bar right in front of my car. I almost ran over him. He got himself into the car and was passed out by the time we got home. It was cold that evening so I just left the car window down and went inside. It was about 2am when I heard the front door of the house open and he came in. He had been unconscious in the car for eight hours. Even though he went to a couple of AA meetings, he would tell me he wasn't like those other people attending. He couldn't see that it was destroying our marriage and my love for him. He could only see as far as his next drink.

A few weeks after this he went back to AA and seemed, for the first time, to recognize that his drinking was causing problems. In order to attend meetings he got, and for a while he kept, a job in Newry in a little restaurant working the lunch shift only, while I was working for a disability rights organization also in Newry. This way he could leave work and attend a meeting before walking to my office and we would drive home together.

Things improved between us and we began trying for a family, but nothing was happening. After several months trying both of us went for tests but doctors could find nothing wrong with either of us. So we kept trying. We also applied for the Green Card Visa Lottery which, if we were successful, would allow us to move to the USA. The troubles were still going on in Northern Ireland and if we ever did have children, I did not want them growing up in a situation where they could be dead before their 20th birthday.

Towards the end of 1993, after finding Declan passed out on the street several times both in Newry and Warrenpoint, I decided enough was enough. It was so embarrassing to drive through town and see him passed out on the pavement.

One evening he came home and said he needed to go to the shop. We lived about a mile out of town. I didn't think anything of it when he hadn't come back after 20 minutes or so. But then I happened to glance at the hall table where I left my rings handy to put on going out. My rings were gone and when I looked in my jewellery box so was a gold bracelet he had bought for me in Jersey when we first met. So I called the police and told them my husband had stolen them and that I wanted him arrested for it. The police picked him up going into a bar in the town and kept him overnight. Next morning I got a barring order on him, which did not allow him near me or the house. The police were at the court and gave me back my jewellery. My patience had worn out. I was beginning to wonder if he ever loved me at all, or had just seen me as a handy meal ticket. He didn't seem to understand that it was not okay for him to assume his wages were drinking money while I was left to pay all the bills out of my salary.

After much begging and pleading to come home, and after firm refusals from me, he found a place in the Simon Community in Newry in December 1993. The Simon Community had a large house there where homeless people could get temporary accommodation while they sorted their lives out. He even threatened to commit suicide so that I would take him back but I was becoming stronger emotionally and I told him I would miss him but if he was determined to kill himself there was nothing I could do because he was an adult. He stayed there for three weeks and he called to let me know he had been given an inpatient place in a treatment facility but they couldn't take him until the end of the month, a couple of days after Christmas. However, until then he was attending an outpatient clinic. But I still wondered if he had really started to see that he had a major problem, or if he was agreeing with everyone so that he could get back to the comfortable home and the money available for him to drink again. I agreed to let him come home for a few hours on Christmas Day. That was the hardest Christmas ever. We both knew he was leaving again, and I so badly wanted to let him stay. He pleaded with me not to send him away, but I couldn't trust him to be there and so I drove him back to the Simon Community that night.

He went into treatment in January and after two weeks or so the social worker asked if he could spend the weekends at home because a stable home atmosphere would give him the chance to make a better recovery than while dealing with the stress of being homeless. I agreed on the condition that he wasn't to drink, and so he came home. He was in treatment until April, and on one of his weekends home when relations were getting better between us, I fell pregnant.

I hadn't been feeling very well and went to the doctor. I gave a urine sample and that afternoon, as I was in the office alone—Declan called in to get a lift home—the phone rang and the doctor's receptionist told me I was pregnant. I put the phone down and asked Declan what he thought about being a daddy. He was overjoyed. From that moment on right through my pregnancy he never drank, continued with his meetings, and found another job in Newry, at the Golf Club. He was working fewer hours, as recommended by his doctors, so that he could attend AA meetings and outpatient sessions. At one of the outpatient sessions his doctor told me he wished us well but he didn't believe that Declan had been totally honest about the cause of his drinking and he was too interested in other people's recovery to be totally invested in his own. I hoped she was wrong but I kept a careful watch nevertheless.

After waiting what seemed like a lifetime since we had applied for the visa program, we received a letter to attend the American Embassy in London in May 1994. We drove over and the interviews and medicals—which consisted of a blood test to check for HIV—were finished very quickly. Our holiday visas were taken from our passports and we were issued temporary green cards. In order to get temporary Green Cards we needed a letter from an employer stating that one of us had a full-time job to go to. Declan got a letter from a fellow chef who partly owned a restaurant in Connecticut and the Embassy was happy with this. We were told we had to enter the USA within 12 weeks of the interview date, but we could leave again as long as we were back there within one year. I was four months pregnant so we made arrangements fairly quickly.

We researched different parts of the US and decided that we would check out Texas. From what we read, Dallas and Houston were too large and had a lot of gang problems, whereas the capital, Austin, was smaller and didn't seem to have the same level of gang activity or the humidity suffered by the other two cities. Austin was intriguing in that it had a huge fruit bat population that lived under one of the bridges in the centre of the city. There also seemed to be a low unemployment rate. I called the Independent Living Centre there and found out that public transport was wheelchair accessible and there were good employment opportunities for everyone, including people with disabilities. Texas was so large we decided that if we didn't like Austin there were lots of other towns and cities to look into. Another bonus was that the weather was good most of the year. This was important because Declan, as a result of a motorcycle accident years before, was beginning to feel the effects of arthritis in his hands when the weather was cold and damp.

I wanted a fresh start and Declan to be removed from all the influences I thought were triggers to his drinking. I wanted to attend college to get a degree, while Declan would eventually be able to open his own restaurant and be his own boss, something he dreamed of.

On the flight to Texas I felt my baby move for the first time. It was like a little butterfly fluttering its wings in my stomach. The love I already felt for this little person-to-be was incredible.

We arrived in Austin, Texas and took a cab from the airport to the downtown accessible hotel we had booked. I was so excited and amazed at the tall buildings all lit up; the University of Texas tower was bathed in orange. It was all so American…and this would be the start of our new life.

People had told me the buses were wheelchair friendly but I had trouble believing I would ever be able to ride a bus alone. However, we got up next day and went to look around and sure enough all the buses were accessible to wheelchairs.

During our first week there we went and applied for social security numbers. We also checked out the housing situation and even had a look at the papers for employment, to give us some idea of wages and house prices for when we came back for good.

On the bus one day, going to a shopping mall, we met a young woman who used a wheelchair. She was very friendly and her name was Jennifer. She gave us a business card and told us we should come visit them —ADAPT— before we went home. ADAPT stands for American Disabled Accessible Programs Today. The group is based on the idea that people with disabilities should have the same rights as everyone else in all areas of life.

A couple of days later we took Jennifer up on her offer and went to their offices. I learned that these people were not always happy that companies would try to get around the Americans with Disabilities Act, and so when this happened ADAPT people would show up and chain themselves to buildings, under buses, etc, to highlight the injustice. They had all been to jail several times for civil disobedience offences. They were my kind of people.

We also met a guy called Ed who worked at the Independent Living Center. He was visually impaired and had given us lots of information over the phone on where to stay, housing, transportation and employment prospects before we had arrived in Texas. We brought him some Irish tapes because he said he was into music. He invited us over to his house for a barbeque and by the end of the evening he had offered to let our actual green cards be sent to his address and he would forward them to us. The rules on the green card were that you had to have a permanent address in the US for the cards to be mailed to you, and although we would be able to leave the country without them, we wouldn't be allowed to re-enter without them.

As we weren't able to open a bank account, or apply for ID cards without social security numbers, we decided to take a cheap five-day trip to Las Vegas to kill some time.

We visited the Grand Canyon in a little 12-person plane and also saw the Hoover Dam. I was halfway through my pregnancy so I had to rest. I spent a lot of time sitting on the pool steps because I was afraid that it was so hot there that the baby would literally boil inside me.

Back in Austin our social security cards were waiting for us and so next day we went straight to the bank and opened an account. Declan sat the driving test too and passed first time. I couldn't do that without a specialized car so I got an ID in the meantime, until we moved and I could get a car. We flew to Houston to visit TIRR, Texas Institute of Rehabilitation and Research, to meet with their driving people and see what sort of controls I would need to allow me to drive there. After meeting with them, and having a test drive in their van, I decided that I would be able to drive using regular hand controls. The only other alterations I would need would be a swivel seat and a van with either a lift or a lowered floor. It was going to be expensive but worth it. I had never driven a van with a lift or been able to actually bring my chair into a car before. I was very excited at this prospect.

We also visited a medical supplies store and I tested out several of the powered wheelchairs there. I fell in love with the faster, more robust chairs and decided, seeing as they were a third of the price of the chairs back home, to buy one. This chair was great—suddenly I could go for 12-15 miles on one charge and it had little wheels at the back which meant I could go up small footpaths—and it looked great! It also came with an international charger which meant I could now take my chair anywhere I wanted to go. On top of this the top speed was 8mph which meant when our child started to run I could keep up with them, or stay alongside them when they were riding their bike or roller blading. Because the chair had to be ordered I got the slightly startled owner to agree to ship the chair to me in Ireland. Customs waived charges as I persuaded them we were on our way out of the country soon to live in the USA and so, really, the chair was in transit.

At the end of the three weeks we flew back and began organizing ourselves for our move to a new life. But my worries about moving to another country with Declan surfaced again on the flight back to Ireland when he got extremely drunk. The bar was free on international flights to the USA and Declan must have managed to drink the bar almost dry while I slept. I was mortified when the airline staff had to give him smelling salts to wake him when we landed. He was belligerent to the airline staff and they would have called the airport police if Declan had not left the aircraft when he did.

We had decided to stay in Dublin for the night because after the overnight flight, and being pregnant, I thought I would be too tired to try to drive home. I regretted this decision because by the time we had made it to our hotel room in Dublin he was extremely argumentative and threatened that he would 'see to me and the baby' if I didn't leave him alone and let him drink at the hotel bar that day. I stayed out of his way and he soon passed out. Of course there were the 'I love you' and apologies the next morning—but another little piece of my love had been killed and a sleepless night had been spent wondering how I would cope with his baby alone if I ended up leaving him. One thing was for certain, with or without Declan I was moving to Texas where things would be more accessible and offer me a better chance at bringing up my child. I knew that I would have to set myself up with a support network as soon as possible in Texas because it was very obvious that if I couldn't trust him on a flight, then I could never trust that he would be there for me or my child when we were living so far from home.

I understand now why battered women stay quiet about their abuse and don't leave their tormentor. I never told my family or Declan's family about his behaviour. Looking back I can only think it was because I was ashamed I had failed at marriage. I wasn't angry enough then. I still believed that if I did things differently then he wouldn't drink and everything would be okay. After all, when he was sober he was a lovely man and very loving and helpful.

Can I be an Independent Mom?

Most new mothers worry about things: will they be good mothers; will their babies cry all night or sleep? My worries throughout my pregnancy were about whether I would be able to feed, dress, carry, change and generally care for my baby independently. I also worried whether the baby, as they got older, would get teased or bullied because of their mom being different.

I also knew that I could no longer rely on Declan and at some point I would probably be a single parent.

But still I loved every minute of being pregnant. I changed my diet to eat fruit, meat and vegetables, and the only pills I took were iron and folic acid. My skin glowed and my hair was in better condition than it had ever been. I was on a happy high for the nine months.

Pregnancy brought some problems too. As my stomach grew I had to give up jumping on the trampoline for exercise, which I did one night a week at the Sports Centre in Newry. I also had to learn to do things differently as I couldn't pull myself in or out of the bath on my stomach, and as I was walking at the time on little boots, I had to be extremely careful. I also couldn't pull myself in and out of my wheelchair any more, and so needed someone to come with me when I went shopping, or else have the security men at the shopping centre take my chair out of the car and bring it round to the door of the car for me.

During my first 14 weeks of pregnancy I was scanned more than a half dozen times because the doctor wanted to be sure that the baby's arms and legs were growing okay. Even though my disability was not genetic the doctor was holding his breath that everything would be okay. I, surprisingly enough, didn't have those worries. I had seen Maggie having two sturdy boys and other thalidomide women give birth to regular, healthy children so I never expected anything different for us. As my pregnancy progressed the doctor was excited that the baby was sitting correctly but even so we decided on a caesarian birth because of the damage already done to my pelvis by my disability.

At seven months pregnant I visited the maternity ward and met the nurses who would care for me. I had been given a hydraulic bath seat worked by pressurised air, which sat in the bath and could raise me to my chair level or lower me into the bath. The staff on the maternity ward decided that rather than have to lift it in and out of the bath each time another woman wanted to use the bath, they would put me in a private room with its own bathroom.

During my whole pregnancy, apart from the flight back from America, Declan had remained sober. He regularly rubbed my stomach and talked to the baby who we had nicknamed Bubble. We knew it was going to be a little boy, and after weeks of thinking of different names, we decided to call him Karl. We chose the name because it could be associated with neither the Protestant nor Catholic religions. It sounds silly, I know, but at that time in Northern Ireland people's religion could be determined by their name, and that very often led to someone being shot, or not having freedom of movement because they were afraid to go into the wrong area and be fingered because of their name.

I drove right up until the day I went into hospital. The week before I gave birth I drove to Belfast to do all the Christmas shopping, wrapped everything and put the presents under the tree because I knew I couldn't do it when I came home. It was much easier to carry the baby in me than on me.

I was prepared too with all the baby paraphernalia, some of which was adapted for my needs. The cot was converted with the cot side cut in half so rather than the side of it dropping down to lift the baby out, mine opened out in the middle like two little doors. There was a lock on the top and bottom so Karl could not push it open and fall out once he was big enough to sit or stand. The cot legs were also lengthened to provide a better height for me to lift him. I had a changing table made to the correct height for me and covered with a washable surface.

I went into hospital on 15 December 1994. I met with the anaesthetist because he was nervous about giving me the right quantities of anaesthetic and also wanted to talk me through the procedure. I had to have blood tests in case I needed a transfusion after the birth. The rest of the day I spent just hanging around, visiting the other women on the ward, reading and getting more and more anxious by the minute. Questions like *will I be able to carry him, how will I change him, will he get teased because of me* kept going around in my head. I was already hurt by some friends, and strangers too, when they questioned me as to whether I should be having a baby at all. Was I not entitled to that experience either because of my disability?

That night I didn't sleep at all. I was so excited about what he would look like. I talked to him all night, rubbing my belly as best I could to reassure the baby everything would be just fine. I talked to him about the fun we would have when he was older, and about our new life in America.

I didn't reach the operating room until about 1.30pm because the theatres were in use due to a multiple accident. I already had a butterfly needle put in my hand the day before but when I went to theatre I was given pink stuff to drink to stop heartburn and reflux. Then an oxygen mask was placed on my face and I was given pure oxygen to breathe for five minutes to try to negate the effects of the anaesthetic on the baby. Declan came with me and was allowed into theatre to witness the birth of our son.

I was wheeled in and put on the table and the anaesthetic was put into the butterfly needle in my hand. I fell asleep and it seemed like only minutes later I was being told to wake up. I opened my eyes and asked to see the baby. He was in a bassinet behind me and the nurse carried him around for me to see. I looked at him and was amazed I had produced this amazing, perfect little human. I loved him immediately. I fell asleep again and when I woke I asked the same thing. Then, exhausted but exhilarated, I fell asleep again. After doing this three times the nurse told me Karl was starving from all the exercise and they were going to take him up to the nursery. I insisted Declan went with him because although I had just seen Karl for a moment the love I felt for this tiny bundle was nothing I'd ever felt before. My love for him hurt more (in a good way) than the surgery, and I was terrified that someone would snatch him because he was so beautiful.

Once Declan and Karl were gone, the nurses told me they would freshen me up before taking me back to the ward. Someone had told me before the birth that moving as soon as possible after the surgery stopped you stiffening up and would make the recovery faster. So I had the nurses gently sit me up a little and lay me down again. Then they washed my face and called the porters to push me in my bed back to the ward. On the way back to the ward I was wheeled into an elevator that visitors also used. I told everyone in the elevator about my baby, and informed them all, apparently, that I did it all myself. I was so proud to be a mom I was floating on air, although that might also have been helped by the anaesthetic, which was wearing off, and the morphine I had been given.

As soon as I was settled—I was attached to a morphine drip and had a catheter so I didn't need to move too much for the rest of the day—Declan came in holding Karl. He laid him in my arms and I fell asleep, happy that I was a mom but oblivious to the changes that would force me to be able to care for him like I never expected I could.

I was in hospital for eight days after Karl's birth. For the first day I rested and was given Karl to hold while lying in the bed. I also got rid of the drip and the catheter and slowly, with help, managed to get into my wheelchair and have a wander around the maternity unit. But I was still very concerned about how much I would be able to do for Karl independently.

A couple of days after I gave birth the ward sister came in and told me she had figured out how I could lift, change and feed Karl unaided. I was thrilled but scared as she talked me through how I could grasp the front of his babygro with my teeth and gently swing him up onto my shoulder from the bed. After practicing a few times I got the hang of it—and Karl didn't seem particularly bothered about all this moving around. Then I learned how I could, with a bench at the correct height, change his nappy, and by propping him on a pillow and supporting his head with one hand, I could feed him.

We got out of the hospital on Christmas Eve. Our taxi driver—Sean the taxi who drove the only wheelchair accessible taxi in Newry—took us home. He wouldn't take any money for the fare—he said it was his gift for the baby.

The Christmas tree was switched on, the house was warm and Karl was asleep. For about 5 minutes it seemed like the perfect family setting; then Karl woke up and started screaming. We tried holding him, feeding him, changing him, singing to him; but he was still screaming at 11pm when I called the hospital and asked what to do. The nurse told me to switch on the vacuum next to his carry cot. I thought she was nuts but it worked! She told me it was the same type of white noise as he heard in the womb and so it soothed him. We burned out a few hairdryers and almost burned out the vacuum cleaner during the next several weeks.

We set about a routine the next day. Karl, because he was small, needed to be fed every three hours and so I would go to bed after his 8pm feed and sleep until 7am. Declan would feed him at 11pm and then again in the middle of the night, and then he would sleep on until close to lunchtime. He was off work except at the weekends in the Golf Club, so the arrangement worked well at the time. I developed 'baby blues' and so the doctor ordered me to rest and let Declan take more responsibility.

When people talk of baby blues you think that someone is perhaps a little weepy. But I got to the stage of truly believing that if I killed myself Karl and Declan would be better off. I even planned how to do it. I was going to drive off the end of the docks in Warrenpoint. Luckily a midwife who came to visit spotted that something was wrong and called the doctor, who kept a close watch on me for a few weeks until it passed. Friends came to visit and Maggie came from Galway and was a great help, showing me how she did different things for her boys. People who have regular length arms would have found it more difficult to think of innovative ways around the problems a new mom might encounter.

I was off work for another 12 weeks, and so I set about becoming a mom. Karl was a good baby and by eight weeks old he was sleeping through the night. The midwife had told me at eight weeks to give him a tiny taste of mixed up baby rice on the end of a spoon right before his last feed. The first night I did it he slept for 12 hours and I was certain that he had died. I kept poking him to make sure he was breathing.

BY THE TIME I WENT BACK TO WORK IN APRIL WE HAD already put plans in motion for moving to Texas. We had booked the removal firm—we were taking all our furniture with us and so would be without furniture for three weeks before we left and 3 weeks in the USA. We had also bought the tickets for the flights—the plan being that Declan would go out three weeks before Karl and I, get a car on the road and also find us an apartment to live in. He was supposed to start job hunting then too.

During this time I would finish working out my notice, finalise renting out our house and organize getting rid of everything that was left behind before we left. My sister Anne became Karl's carer during the day when I was at work, and because we had no pots, pans or dishes left behind, I ate at her house in the evenings on my way home from work.

I often wondered what my own mother would have thought of my current situation. I know she would have been so proud that I was a mother myself, and it made me smile to think she probably would have been freaking out at the thought of me moving to a different country with a baby and an alcoholic, minus a support network.

THE CURSE OF ALCOHOLISM

I HAD DEVELOPED A FALSE SENSE OF SECURITY OVER the pregnancy and with Declan's drinking problem. At the beginning of May I came home from work one evening to find Declan drunk and passed out on the sofa, holding Karl in his arms. Karl was crying and it took a bit of effort but eventually I managed to get him from Declan. Once I had him settled I woke Declan and told him if he ever got drunk minding Karl again I was going to the police to have him charged with child endangerment. He was very apologetic and assured me it had never happened before and that he had learnt his lesson and it wouldn't happen again. But I had lost my trust in him, and so on days when I could not keep ringing him from the office, I arranged for Karl to be with my sister—just to be sure.

I was aware that I was probably making a mistake moving to a strange country where I knew nobody, had no support and no job, and because Declan was drinking again. But over the next few weeks he seemed fine, and I didn't detect any drink on his breath. Karl was growing fast, and even learning how to roll and push himself up on his hands.

The furniture company came and packed up around the middle of June. All we had left was a bed, the fridge, kitchen table and an armchair borrowed from one of the neighbours. Declan flew out a couple of days later. I was very concerned when I didn't hear from him for almost two days. He told me it was because he didn't know how to make international calls on the hotel phone—and the hotel he was at was a cheap one anyway. However, within two weeks he had bought a little secondhand car, and found us an apartment in a complex called Pecan Grove. He also called—or I called him—every day so I thought our troubled times had passed. I desperately wanted to believe we were starting a brilliant new life together. However, I wasn't factoring in the time differences between the two countries and when I spoke to him it was his afternoon—plenty of time after our calls for him to drink, as I discovered from neighbours at the apartment complex at a much later date, when after we had split up they told me about having to carry him from the pool to the apartment most nights.

My friend Anne, from the Tech, was now married with three children, and two days before we left for Texas she had her fourth—a little boy. I went to visit her in hospital the evening before we left, and had my last meal in Ireland with her husband Liam after the visit. I watched Anne and Liam together and had serious doubts, even then, whether Declan and I would ever be that happy, and whether I could ever trust him the way Anne was able to trust Liam to be there for her when she needed him.

That night I could barely sleep from the excitement and trepidation at what I was doing. What if things didn't work out? What if Declan started drinking again? Were we doing the right thing? How would I cope with a baby if things didn't work out?

I left our home in Warrenpoint for the last time on 2 July 1995. My niece, Tina, was flying over to Texas with Karl and I to help me feed and change him on the flights. We stopped off to say goodbye to my sister and her family, and then we were off to Dublin airport.

We arrived at the airport and checked in. The airline people were very nice and organized for Karl to have a bassinet for the flight. Then we went through security and on to US immigration. The man at immigration looked at my passport and temporary green card and

I had my fingerprints taken for verification of who I was. Then he told me that I could go on the flight with no problem but Karl had no paperwork and so would have to stay behind. I explained that I had been pregnant when issued with the temporary visa and was told he would be sorted when we arrived in the USA. The man was little jobs-worth guy (you know the sort: 'more than my job's worth'). There was no budging him so I asked him to hold Karl for a second. Then I reached to the back of my chair, took his baby bag off, handed it to the man and kissed Karl on the forehead. I then proceeded to tell him that there were enough nappies and bottles to last until the next morning but after that he was on his own until he could get my child to me in Texas. I pointed out he would have to take responsibility because at six months old, Karl was far too young to travel back North on his own.

The look on his face was a picture. About 10 seconds passed and I held my breath, not knowing what he would do. He handed Karl back to me and told me he would make a call and arrange an appointment to get Karl his green card in Texas. He wished us well and very quickly got rid of us out of his office.

After a brief stop-over in Atlanta, Georgia I saw the lights of Austin beneath the plane. Butterflies exploded in my belly as I dreamed of the new life we were embarking on. My son would grow up in sunshine and my husband would one day own his own restaurant. I would go back to college and get a degree and we would live a wonderful life together.

We were the last off the plane, but the airport people let Declan on the flight to us after he explained we were emigrating and he hadn't seen us for three weeks. There was something different about him. It felt to me that he was glad to see us, but not glad in the way that someone who had been without his baby for so long would have been, instead happy in a way that someone would be if they were glad to see visitors who were only going to stay for a while. That really worried me, but not as much as I worried when Declan took us to our new home. It was an apartment in a complex. The apartment was very nice with two bedrooms, but when I opened the huge fridge in the kitchen and found two 24 packs of beer there, I knew we were in major trouble. When I asked Declan about it, he told me he wasn't drinking heavily, and he could handle it—I think I knew better!

When I met Delores she was 68 years old. She weighed about 300lb and walked into our apartment using a cane. She told me she had fallen a couple of years earlier and damaged her knee. She was so full of life—her husband had died several years earlier and she had decided that, after caring for him for seven years since his stroke, she was going to live. She went on cruises alone, and everyone she met immediately fell in love with her. I was no different.

Delores lived in the apartment next door and she introduced herself to us by bringing Karl a lovely blue and white knitted teddy bear that she had made. She had loaned Declan a bed for Karl's room, some lawn chairs to sit on, and a long fold-up table for us to eat from, until our own furniture arrived. I liked her instantly, and as she picked Karl up she told me her grandchildren had all grown up and she needed a baby in her life, so she became 'Nanny' to Karl and later to Aisling.

On 4 July, Independence Day and a huge holiday in the USA, we went on the bus to the lake in town to see the fireworks display. It was a beautiful evening and the display was amazing, like a welcome to our new homeland. But later that evening we discovered it's not so easy to get home when thousands of people are trying to do the same thing. Tina and I ended up walking to a downtown hotel and calling a wheelchair taxi, while Declan managed to catch a regular taxi and take Karl back to the apartment to change him, feed him and put him to bed.

A couple of days later our troubles really began when Declan tried to pick an argument. I wouldn't play the game, so he went into the bedroom and appeared several minutes later all dressed up. He announced he was going out, and left in the car. He didn't come home that night—or the next—so next morning, Monday, I went to the bank as soon as it opened and took all the money, except for $40, and moved it to a different bank. I opened an account in my name only.

On Tuesday morning Declan arrived home as if nothing had happened. I asked Tina to take Karl for a walk, and then I told Declan that he either get his act together and start attending AA again and get a job, or else he could just leave. He was no use to me as he was. I also told him I would start to look for a job shortly and find Karl a place at daycare. He promised me he was sorry and that it wouldn't happen again. Then he asked about our money and I told him I was in charge of it now. That was probably the only reason he came home.

Tina left a few days later. She had an offer of a paid internship in England and decided to take it. The day she left I really wondered about what the hell I had done. I was living with an alcoholic in a non-accessible apartment without any family support. I could look after Karl there to a degree, but I couldn't use the cooker, or reach the sink in the kitchen to wash up, and I couldn't bathe Karl alone. I also wondered whether Tina would be relieved to be away from the tension of living with an out of control alcoholic and that's why she had gone so soon. I couldn't really blame her.

Once Tina had gone, I knew I needed to get accessible transportation for myself. I saw an ad for a used Ford van and I went to see it. I bought the van and had minor modifications done to the hand controls—it already had a lift on the side. Now I could take driving lessons and pass the Texas driving test.

One of our neighbours would come driving with me on Sundays and I passed my test within a couple of weeks. This left me independent of Declan and able to transport Karl myself. Because it was a big mini-bus type van I had enough room inside to drive my chair in and lift Karl in and out of his car seat on my own.

A few weeks after we arrived in Texas, and thinking that because there was an Americans with Disabilities Act that made me just like everyone else, I went looking for work. I went to my first Temp Agency. Looking back now I can only wonder what the young girl was thinking when I breezed into their offices and told her I was looking for work. All she had to go on right then was my appearance. She was very professional though and asked what I could do. I told her anything administrative or clerical would be fine. She asked me to take a typing test and before I took it asked what programs I used in Ireland. Seeing as I had worked for the voluntary sector and the only program used was DOS, I told her I didn't know because they all had different names in Ireland. I was sweating it that I would make a fool of myself but when I saw all the little icons at the top of the Word screen I managed to fake my way through it and had a high enough score that she said she would be in touch when something came up.

She called me back the next day to see if I was interested in a job as a data entry operator. Having no clue what this was I told her that I would take it. I got Karl a place in daycare close by where I worked, and Declan was actively looking for a job. He found a chef position in a restaurant in the middle of Austin. It was handy because there was a bus stop right outside our apartment and one close to his workplace. This meant he didn't have to take the car to work and worry about where to park. As for my own new job, when I went to the company I was happy to discover it was just entering names, addresses and other details onto forms. It was an easy job but didn't pay well. However, I was now working in my new country, just like everyone else.

Declan seemed to settle into his new job too. Then one Sunday evening he left to go to Threadgills restaurant up the road to get us some dinner. I didn't go with him because Karl was teething and not in good form. He should have been gone about 20 minutes or so, but three hours later there was still no sign of him. Later that evening I got a phone call from Declan to say he'd been arrested. I asked to speak to an officer and asked what had happened. Apparently he had gotten really drunk and run into several parked cars, wrecking his own car in the process. He was not hurt but still very drunk. He was put back on the phone again and demanded that I come bail him out. I refused, realizing that I didn't love him anymore and didn't want to live like this. The officer also advised me that he would be released the next morning after he had seen the judge. In the meantime I had a baby I needed help with to get up and fed the next morning. Once again Delores came to the rescue. She told me then that I needed to find a house, have it adapted for me, and I needed to leave Declan before he dragged us down with him.

The next day, Declan was back at home, and went straight into work in a job he had secured as a chef in Louis 106—a fashionable downtown restaurant. He sobered up, and was court ordered to attend AA every day. He also had to see a counsellor once a week for his drinking issues. This worked well for a couple of months until I discovered I was pregnant again around Christmas time.

That Christmas we were still living in the apartment. We bought a tree and decorated it, and Karl was bought presents both by us and by Delores, who I had come to rely on as my surrogate mother. Our friend Aidan came over from Belfast and was with us as well. It was a good day and one to remember.

However, on New Year's Eve, while Aidan was still with us, Declan bought a bottle of wine for Aidan and I to share. He was still sober and seemed to be doing well. But I could only take a mouthful of the wine before I felt sick—I knew that feeling and got a pregnancy kit the next day. It was positive.

Declan was working and attending his meetings. He had been sober for three months and we were getting on much better until I discovered I was pregnant again. I rang him at work to break the good news. He sounded stunned—and then he didn't come home until very late that night. He was drinking again.

Delores was thrilled about the pregnancy. I was happy but concerned knowing that I may have to deal with two babies alone. I was determined that I was going to divorce him if he went off the rails again

On Valentine's night, Delores had offered to babysit so that we could go for a meal together and maybe see a movie. So while Declan changed Karl into his pyjamas, I went to the 7-11 store across the road to get some milk for breakfast in the morning. I went onto the crossing just as the green man started to flash and next thing I knew I was lying in the hospital. Apparently I had been hit by a car that had not stopped for the crossing. Declan, I discovered later, was told by a neighbour who knocked on the door, and he then rushed Karl to Delores and followed the ambulance in our van. I was x-rayed and scanned, but had no broken bones. I needed stitches in my face and the back of my head, and because I was pregnant I was kept in hospital so they could monitor the baby and make sure no damage had happened that would cause a miscarriage. I was semi-conscious for a day or so and was in hospital for four. Later I discovered that I had only limited feeling in part of my left leg as well.

While in the hospital they asked a to come and talk to me. His name was Bradley Price. Dr Price asked if I had a gynaecologist yet. I told him I had no health insurance so could not afford it. He said that he would be my doctor and if I was denied Medicaid (the state funded medical card) that he would not charge me for his services. They say that God works in mysterious ways—had I not been knocked down I would not have found this doctor who was willing to deliver my baby for free.

When I was discharged from the hospital I was given the loan of a wheelchair until the Thalidomide Trust in England paid for a new one for me. Apparently when the car hit me I flew up into the air and the chair was pushed on down the road by the car. The chair was a write off and the doctor told me I was lucky to have been thrown clear.

When we discovered I was pregnant, we decided we needed to hire a girl to help with Karl at the weekends when Declan was working. We hired a student named Crystal. She was very good with Karl and I was always with her. Having her with me meant we could go to the shopping mall and she would be there if he needed changed or fed. I was able to do these things in my own environment but the changing tables outside the home were too tall for me and I had nowhere to put Karl to feed him. When the weather was good Crystal could also get into the pool with Karl while I watched her.

However, Crystal caused me a world of hurt and made me a little uncomfortable with hiring anyone else when she reported me to Child Protection Services for abandoning my baby in February for four days, leaving him with her when his dad was working.

I could never understand why she did this when she knew that I was in hospital for those days. Declan had explained the situation to her when he asked if she could she work extra hours as he had to go to work himself, and Delores took Karl from her at the end of her work session until Declan came home.

I was only home from the hospital a couple of hours when I got a call from a social worker at Child Protective Services. She told me a complaint had been made that I had abandoned my child and that he had a bad cough and terrible nappy rash. I explained to her that I had been involved in an accident but Karl had been properly cared for in my absence. I also explained that his cough and rash were because he was teething and the doctor had given us cream and told us it was quite normal. I invited the social worker to come on over and see his home for herself. She told me they would check in with the daycare and get back to me. They investigated me and eventually apologized. Crystal had decided to report me because she thought I was unfit to be a mother because of my disability. She even had the neck to show up the following weekend like nothing had happened. I told her I couldn't trust her to be in my home anymore and asked her to leave.

Positive things did happen at this time; it wasn't all negative. I was working for a state agency and was taken on as a regular full-time employee for six months, meaning I now had good medical insurance coverage that would cover the expenses involved in having the baby in hospital

One evening I left Karl with Delores and I went along to a meeting ADAPT was holding. I thought it a good idea to get to know some other people with disabilities living in Austin. At the meeting I did a double take and couldn't help staring in fascination at a guy sitting across from me who didn't have any legs and only had one short arm ending in one finger. He was also staring at me too. For other people it is nothing to meet someone who looks like you, but for someone like me it is always an event to meet a fellow 'thalidomider'. I guessed he was thalidomide-affected because he had the characteristic thalidomide wide nose.

The man's name was John and it turned out that he also had a son, six months younger than Karl. John was also married to someone without a disability. After the meeting we talked and he invited us to visit them.

We went to visit the next week and I was able to show John how he could pick up his son in his teeth and cradle him in his arm. I also showed him how he could feed Joshua using a bottle with handles attached. He decided the nappy changing should still be left to his wife—he had no desire to have his face go so close to a dirty nappy.

Around this same time Declan lost his job through drinking. I would come home in the evening and find him passed out in the apartment, or sometimes on the path leading to the apartment. We had signed a contract for a new house to be built, secured a mortgage, and now were waiting for it to be finished before we could move. Before I went to daycare for Karl I would push Declan into the bedroom and close the door on him in order to protect Karl from seeing his dad like that.

Declan and I obviously weren't getting on because of his drinking. In the US, the owners of a home getting built get to choose the colour of the carpets, tiles for the floors, colour of the kitchen and bathroom cabinets as well. On the day we were to go to the showroom to choose, Declan refused to come with me. That was when I made the decision that sooner or later, preferably sooner, the new house would only be for the children and myself.

Our marriage was over and I was very scared at the thought of being solely responsible for two babies. But I had, and still have great faith and I knew God wouldn't put something my way that I could not find a solution to.

As anyone who has lived with an alcoholic would understand, my routine centred on Declan's drinking; I raced home from work, so that when Karl came home everything would appear normal. I even came home one afternoon to find the apartment full of smoke. Declan had decided to boil water for something, got drunk and passed out. The water had boiled away and there was a hole in the bottom of the pot. He was lying on the kitchen floor and I called an ambulance because I thought he had been overcome by smoke. Turned out it was alcohol and once they gave him oxygen he was okay. Still drunk but okay.

One day I came home exhausted to find Declan sober and dinner ready to be popped into the microwave when we wanted to eat. He offered to go get Karl from daycare and so I let him while I had a nap. The stress of dealing with Declan, combined with the constant nausea I felt for the first trimester of this pregnancy, was exhausting me. I woke up about an hour later and began to panic because they were not home. I called the daycare and was told Karl had been collected a while ago. Then I saw the van pull in and I went outside. Declan lifted Karl out of the van and was staggering down the path with him. I couldn't believe it—he had been drinking on the way home with Karl in the van. I was furious. That was the last time he ever drove my van or had sole responsibility for either child. I had no trust in him anymore, I wanted him gone from our lives but I needed to keep him around until after the baby was born. I didn't feel at all bad at using him—he had been using me to finance his drinking for a long time now.

Declan then began to try to steal money out of my purse while I was asleep. I kept my purse tucked down the side of my chair so it was easy for me to reach but impossible for anyone to steal unless they lifted me first when I was sitting in the chair. I woke one night to find him rooting in my purse for money so that he could sneak out and go to an all-night bar. From then on in I kept the purse in my backpack along with my cheque book, and put it under my pillow when I went to bed.

At the hospital the doctors were concerned about my weight. Even though I was pregnant I wasn't gaining the weight I needed to in order to stay healthy. During my whole pregnancy I had only put on 8lb. I couldn't tell them that It was because I was under so much stress due to working full time, looking after Karl, and not getting a proper night's sleep because my husband would come home drunk late at night, banging on the windows to be let in because he couldn't put the key in the lock. Even going to the laundry room posed a risk because I never knew if it was lies when he said in the evenings he was going to put on a load of laundry or walk out the gates onto a bus for town to drink more. I grew to hate him. I would lie in bed at night and pray he would stagger out into the road and get hit by a car and then my problems would be over.

Declan was put on probation for his drink driving offense. He had to pay $400 a month to the probation department, as well as going to see his probation officer and doing AA classes. One day he decided he wasn't going to pay anymore. He asked to see a judge. On the morning he was due in court I dropped Karl at daycare and came back to the apartment. Even though I was back at the apartment by 8am, Declan, in the 30 minutes he had been awake, had managed to consume a whole bottle of gin and was now sitting on the steps outside the apartment not able to stand and barely able to mumble.

I took him to court anyhow, and the judge ordered that he should serve seven weeks in prison. Declan asked for a treatment program, but he was denied and instead the judge revoked his driving license. The judge told him to turn himself into the police station in two days—on a Saturday—to begin his sentence. I tried to explain to the court officials that my husband was an alcoholic and needed taken into custody right then, as well as needing treatment more than anything, but it fell on deaf ears.

Two days later I dropped Declan off at police headquarters to start serving his sentence. I waited until he went inside. But like any cute alcoholic he waited until I drove off and then left the police station and went drinking. It wasn't until later in the morning that I discovered this, when I called the police station to find out when Declan would be transported to the county prison. He had turned up during the night but they had let him go. However, they told me that if he did not show up by the end of the day a warrant would be issued for his arrest.

I was so frustrated with the system. I left Karl with Delores and went looking for Declan. I found him, lying drunk on the footpath on the next block over from the police station. He was on the footpath with two police cars parked right beside him. The officers were in a local restaurant having their dinner and must have stepped over him to get there from their cars. I got him into my van and then drove to police headquarters. At first they refused to take him to the jail until I threatened them with the press and they became more obliging.

I was living the nightmare of having to put on a happy face for Karl, deal with the stress and shame of Declan being in prison, and of being pregnant, and trying to take care of myself so the baby wouldn't be harmed.

I had to scramble to find someone who would be my PA and help with Karl. A lady called Sandra whom I had gotten to know agreed to work a few hours a day at the weekends and an hour or two in the evenings to bathe Karl for me and help prepare food. It was very difficult living in an apartment that was so inaccessible I could not even reach to work the cooker. I became impatient for word from the builders on our moving in date.

Despite Declan letting me down so terribly, the funny thing was that I still went to the prison on a weekly basis. Behind the glass, talking on the prison phone, he promised me that prison had certainly been a wake-up call and he would turn over a new leaf when he got out.

Right: Leigh, two years old, with Santa.

Below: Leigh, ten years old.

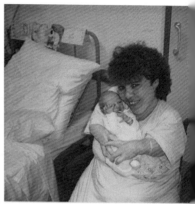

Above right: Leigh at the hospital just after having Karl.

Above left: Leigh at 17.

Below: Leigh with Declan.

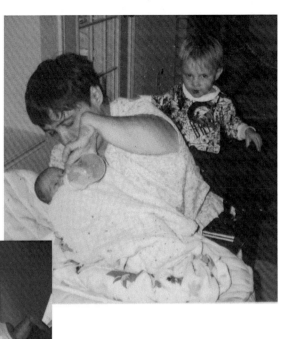

Left: Leigh playing with Karl in their Texas home.

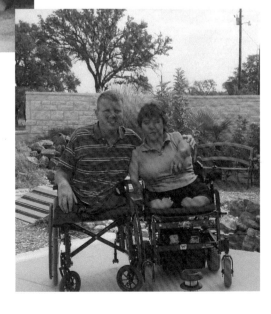

Left: Leigh and Eugene on their wedding day.

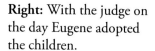

Right: With the judge on the day Eugene adopted the children.

Left: The family (clockwise from Karl, Aisling, Le and Eugene, 201

The Children Must Come First

OUR NEW HOME WAS IN A PART OF THE CITY CALLED Yager Lane. The street was Copperfield Drive. I drove out every day to see the house. The builders were true to their word and we moved in at the end of July as promised.

In the meantime I was trying to hold things together. Delores was my rock of strength and the only one I could confide the situation to. She advised me on a number of occasions to leave him before he killed me—either accidentally or on purpose. She also pointed out to me that it wasn't good for the children to grow up in such an atmosphere. I knew she was right but I was so scared of dealing with the kids alone.

My pregnancy was progressing well. Although I hadn't gained much weight I was relieved that the baby seemed to be healthy and growing accordingly.

Declan got out of prison at the beginning of July and on his way home from the prison, went straight back to the pub. I couldn't leave Karl alone with him when I had the baby so I arranged for my friend Cathy to come over from Ireland with Manus—her son—to be there while I was in hospital and take care of Karl.

We moved from the apartment and into the house at the beginning of August. There were three bedrooms —one for me and one each for the children, as well as a guest room that I would also use as an office. Of course the new baby would be too small to use her own room yet, so it would be a handy storage room at the beginning.

I loved my new house. We took all the furniture from the apartment, and bought anything else that we needed to give us basic comfort. The only thing marring this new life was Declan's drinking. I didn't love him anymore, but I needed him there until the baby was born and then maybe, I naively thought, he would get his act together again and we could be a happy, functional family. But if not, then I had psyched myself up to go it alone. I wasn't sure how, but I could not go on living on edge all the time. Delores was still my rock, but I now had to call her on the phone. I still took Karl to see her regularly.

During the couple of weeks before Aisling was born, Cathy came over and we went to places like Sea World and San Antonio to visit the river walk. Karl loved splashing about in the kiddie section of Sea World and Manus and Cathy could go on the bigger rides. The night before I went to hospital Declan stayed with Manus and Karl while Cathy and I went for a meal. I gave Manus the number of the restaurant and told him to call if Declan took off on them, or seemed to be drinking. Cathy told me her concerns about leaving us when she went home. I told her that I knew my marriage was over. I would lie in bed at night wondering if Declan had ever really loved me, or was it the extra money provided by my disability that he loved? I told her how I had been looking for some way to get a PA to help with the kids when I threw him out but that I had not found a source yet.

I BELIEVE THAT ANGELS COME IN MANY GUISES. DELORES was my guardian angel, always there when I needed a sitter or a shoulder to cry on, or someone to share exciting or happy times with. She loved my children and me. She was like a surrogate mother to me. She got to know our Irish visitors, and it was a running joke that anyone connected to our family had to pass the

Delores test because she was so protective of us. She helped me believe in myself.

Being a first time mom I sought her advice on rashes or fevers Karl developed. I also needed her help in sometimes translating the Texas meaning for things. For example, just after we arrived in Austin, I needed to buy nappies and a dummy for Karl. The people in the grocery store looked at me blankly when I asked for these, so I went back home and showed the items to Delores—discovering from her that a nappy was in fact a 'diaper' and a dummy was a 'pacifier'.

In return for Delores' help and friendship, I would take her shopping or run to the gas station opposite the apartments for milk or bread for her. She had decided when she retired from her job that she was not going to cook anymore, so she ordered her dinner each day from the vast array of fast food restaurants in Austin.

As Declan had lost his license for the drink driving, my friend Paula came and collected us to take us to the hospital for my scheduled C-section.

I was very nervous to be away from Karl, but happy Cathy was there in case Declan started drinking while

I was in the hospital. Declan assured me that he would not be drinking because he was responsible for Karl, but the time for me trusting him had gone. He came with me and was present when I was put to sleep and Aisling was born at 8.02am on Friday, 30 August 1996. But unlike when Karl was born, as soon as Aisling and I were up in the ward, Declan made an excuse to let me rest and he went home.

Cathy came in to see me that evening with Karl and Manus, and she told me Declan had obviously picked up a bottle of vodka on the way back, had come home and said he was going for a shower, but was now lying unconscious in our en-suite bathroom at the house.

On Saturday he came to see me but was very obviously hungover and smelled of stale alcohol. I could hardly wait for him to leave. Unlike when Karl was born we had no plans or dreams to talk about. He knew I no longer loved him and he was putting on a show for the hospital staff—doing what he thought he ought to rather than what he wanted to do.

When I called home during a terrible thunderstorm on Saturday night, he was drunk again and passed out in the bed with Karl this time. I knew then that I had to get my strength back quickly and get him out of our

Don't Tell Me I Can't

lives once and for all. Karl was getting old enough that soon he would be affected by Declan's behaviour and I did not want that for my kids.

Paula came and took me home on the Sunday. While I was getting dressed and ready to go, Declan turned up fairly inebriated, telling the nurses I could do a lot more for myself if I wasn't so damn lazy. I had just had major surgery and yet he thought in his drunken state I should be as mobile as normal. Instead of it being a very happy time, I just wanted to cry.

That night, lying in bed propped up with pillows because I just had surgery two days earlier, when Aisling cried for a feed I had to struggle out of the bed alone, heat her bottle, lift her and feed her. I was in agony but I didn't want to ask Cathy for help. I needed to get used to it because when Cathy went home there was nobody else.

She left for Ireland three days later and so Karl went back to daycare. I needed to keep his routine going for him, plus I needed to sleep when Aisling did so that I could get my strength back and be independent enough to end my sham of a marriage. I still had stitches in my wound, and Declan had to lift me into a bath every morning and then out again. The day after Cathy left he lifted me into the bath and told me he would be

160

back in a few minutes to check on me. I heard the back door close and assumed he had only gone outside for a smoke. Aisling was asleep in her little bassinet, and Karl was at daycare. After a while I realized he had actually left me stranded. I had to pull myself out of the bath, and while doing it I managed to rip a couple of stitches. I was in agony and it took painkillers and about a half hour for me to dress myself and be able to check on Aisling. Fortunately for me, Aisling was also a good baby, blessed with a sunny disposition and had slept through the whole episode.

That was the last straw. I rang an attorney who I had been in contact with to put the wheels in motion to have divorce papers drawn up. Then I went outside to collect the mail. There was something from the bank that I didn't understand and I called them to check. While I was on the phone something in my head clicked and I asked them to check the savings account. They told me my husband had withdrawn $12,000 that morning and there was $3,000 left. I explained to them my husband was not on the account, and so they had no right to give him money on what was a stolen cheque. They agreed to stop the cheque and put the money back into my account.

Life was proving more difficult than I had hoped with two young children and an absent father but I loved them with all my heart and I was determined to do my very best by them. Luckily, this time around I knew how to lift, feed, and change a baby. The only thing I couldn't do was bathe her because I was so afraid of dropping her. So I sponge bathed her on the changing table with her lying on a towel, and then I would gently roll her onto another towel to dry her off.

Even though Aisling was so good I noticed that she seemed to be deaf. In the morning she couldn't hear me coming towards the bassinet but when I leaned over it in her line of vision she would jump like I had startled her. I discussed this with the doctor but when he clapped his hands beside her she reacted so they didn't believe me.

When Declan came home that evening, drunk as usual, I made him go sleep it off in what would be Aisling's room. In the morning I told him I had been to the police over him taking the money and had gotten a protection order which would go into effect on Monday morning. I told him he had until then to pack and go or the police would be around to remove him. Declan told me that half of the savings were his (even though he rarely contributed to the household expenses) and that he had just taken what he was owed. He gave no thought to the fact that I couldn't work for a few weeks after surgery, or that he wasn't working and a mortgage had to be paid and his children fed and clothed from the savings money. The fact he could only think of himself and his own needs made me realize that I was doing the right thing in divorcing him.

On Monday morning I drove Declan to the middle of Austin and left him there. I didn't care if he had nowhere to go—he was inventive enough to get alcohol so let him be inventive enough to sort this out too. Part of me still wanted to shake him until he came to his senses and saw that this was the beginning of the end for us. Why could he not understand that he was about to lose his children and throw away all the opportunities afforded him in this new country?

As soon as I went home I called one of my neighbours who came over and helped me change the front and back door locks. I also called the alarm company and had the burglar alarm activated.

Declan somehow, after two days on the streets, managed to get himself a place in a rehab hospital. They kept him for 10 days and during that time he was detoxed, and a social worker helped find him an apartment. I agreed to pay the first month's rent but made it clear I didn't want him moving back with us. I also made it clear I would be paying no more bills for him, so he better find a way to support himself. I told him he could see the children whenever he liked, but he needed to call me first so that I would know if he was sober.

In the meantime I had to try to keep my family together. Spending the first nights alone with my children was frightening. I had the house alarm activated but I still worried that someone might think we were an easy target. I also worried that Declan might get drunk and decide that he should have the children and try to take them from me. I had to warn the daycare that nobody was to collect them except me, unless they heard otherwise directly from me. I worried about where I would get the money from to continue to pay the mortgage and feed and clothe my family. I prayed—letting God know I was doing my best but needed some help to get the mortgage together each month. My faith was rewarded. Each month the mortgage money would be there—sometimes from the most unexpected sources. For instance, one month a cheque arrived from Ireland. I had sold our house in Warrenpoint, paid off the mortgage and they sent me the remainder of the money from an insurance policy designed to act as a savings account but pay off the mortgage if either of us died. However, because the mortgage was paid, I got the balance. The money was enough to ensure that we got through at least another six months.

In order for me to do all the things like dressing, feeding and getting ready for work, I got up at 5.15am every day. I got Aisling up first. I sponge bathed her on her special changing table, then dressed and fed her a bottle. I sat her in her little baby seat and woke Karl. I changed his nappy and dressed him. I put their little socks on by lying them on the bed, holding up the little foot and gently pulling the socks on with my teeth. Then I put on their little shoes and did the velcro straps with my teeth. I always tried to buy shoes with velcro straps back then. I fed him breakfast and washed his face and then we were off. I dropped the kids at daycare around 6.45am and was in work for 7am. My job at this time was working for Harris Publishing, trying to sell alumni directories over the phone. I hated the job but my self esteem was low and I didn't think I would be able to do anything else. All my dreams of being able to go to college and get a degree were gone. Now I was just trying to earn enough to feed us.

In the evenings I would race over to collect the kids, bring them home and feed them. We ate a lot of fast food because I didn't have the time or energy to cook proper dinners for Karl. Aisling was only two months old so still on bottles. After I fed them I would play with Karl for a little while, and then put on a video tape of Barney for them while I cleared away, put on laundry, ate a little myself and opened the mail. Then I would get them ready for bed, give Karl a sponge bath and get him in his pyjamas. After he was asleep I would give Aisling her last feed and put her down. Then I would pay bills, dry and fold the laundry, sterilize the bottles and make up eight for the following day. I would eventually fall into bed myself at around midnight.

I was exhausted. There was never a break. A few months later out of the blue Declan called and told me he had a job, was sober, and could he come over and help with the kids. I agreed that he could come over after work two evenings a week and get the last bus back to town. He also came over Saturday afternoon and stayed Saturday night in the guest room so he could get up with the kids Sunday morning and give me a rest.

This arrangement was a good one and suited us both. I didn't need to worry whether or not he was drinking because he didn't live with us, and the kids still got to see their daddy. Aisling was really too young to know, but Karl loved his dad and would wait patiently for him on the days he was due. I knew Declan was trying but I didn't trust him. When he stayed over I still slept with the backpack in the bed with me, containing a cheque book, purse and anything else worth stealing. I didn't tell him the alarm code and I had the PIN number on my ATM card changed.

One day I applied for a job with the City of Austin. The job was Intake Officer. The person who got the job would take details of people who came looking for housing, or food stamps or other help the City may give them. It was a job I could easily do and I certainly had enough experience working with people with disabilities before I came to Texas to be able to handle whoever came in.

The application form asked nothing about disability and so I didn't mention I had one. I was selected for interview and went along. I knew by the look on their faces that the two interviewers, who were probably in their 60s, were horrified that someone like me should apply for the job and several times during the interview they told me it was a busy office and nobody would be able to 'carry' the person who got the job. After being told this several times I asked them were they saying this to all the candidates or just me? They looked a little concerned then because the law in the USA forbids discrimination based on disability. But then one of them asked if I would require any 'reasonable accommodations' should I get the job. I told them so long as there was enough space for my chair to get around the office and they had a wheelchair accessible toilet, then no problem.

I didn't hear back from them. I was advised by a friend to make a complaint to the Equal Opportunities Employment Commission. I did and a few months later, after they had completed their investigations, I received a letter of apology from the City, an assurance that they had changed their policies and procedures for interviewing, an assurance the staff in question had been reprimanded for their handling of the interview, and more importantly I received a cheque for the wages I would have earned in the months since the interview had I got the job. That money saw us through another couple of months.

During Christmas 1996, both Declan and Delores stayed over. I had lots of help putting out the presents once the kids were in bed, and again Declan slept in what would eventually be Aisling's room. The next morning we got up and Aisling gave us her usual big smile. To my amazement she had four teeth, two on top and two on bottom. She was only 4 months old so it was a super surprise. Karl had only turned two but he had the Santa thing down, and was really excited when he discovered all his toys. Delores had bought them three presents each (from Santa of course) because she said she liked to give three presents because there were three wise men at the stable in Bethlehem. Even though Declan was there that Christmas, I didn't really feel he was a proper part of our family anymore because I knew come Christmas night he would be gone again.

One night in early March 1997 Declan called on the phone to ask me out. He said he had gotten a bonus at work, and although he should pay off other things he wanted his family back and would like to take me on a date. I agreed providing he organized the babysitter. That Saturday evening Delores arrived at the house with Declan in a taxi. She was going to spend the night to allow us to go out.

Declan first took me to the movies, allowing me to choose what we watched. We saw *George of the Jungle* together and went to the San Francisco Steakhouse for our dinner. As I looked across the table at him, I realized any love I had for Declan had died and I no longer wanted him in my life. It was like sitting across from a stranger. We were polite to each other but I was just numb. Then he told me he thought we had been apart long enough and that I should allow him to move back home. I very adamantly told him that he was to show me a year's sobriety before we could talk seriously about him moving back in. I didn't want him back. I knew that I liked living alone with the kids, I was lonely but at least I knew what was waiting for us when I opened the door in the evening and I was afraid that if he ever moved back in, then I would never get him out, if and when he started drinking again. I never wanted him back in my bed. I felt in control of my life again and didn't want to go back to living on the edge.

Declan came over as usual one evening the next week. Even though he fed and bathed the kids, he seemed jittery and I asked if he was drinking again. He denied it but said that he really needed to go to an AA meeting that night. I wondered then if maybe he was using drugs. It was St Patrick's Day and the temptation was great for him to drink. He left at about 8pm to catch the last bus into town. Karl stood beside me at the front door in his little pyjamas and waved to his dad. That was the last time we ever saw him.

When Declan didn't show for the next two visits I began to suspect he was drinking again, or even using drugs. Hearing my son cry for his daddy on the nights he was supposed to have visited nearly broke my heart. I decided I could wait no longer. Declan would never change. It was all about himself—but I had to put my children first. So I contacted my attorney and with money I could ill afford to spend, directed him to finalize my divorce. Knowing my circumstances, the attorney waived his fees. He also suggested that he put in the decree that I was not responsible for any debts incurred by Declan since our separation.

About two weeks later Declan's landlady called me and asked me to come remove his stuff from the apartment because he was late with the rent and she hadn't seen him in over a week. I told her to call the police in case something untoward had happened and I would meet them at the apartment.

When we entered we found a strange sight. The ironing board was set up and a half ironed shirt was on it. On the sofa were other clothes waiting to be ironed, and on the bed were shirts and pants that were ironed and on hangers, just waiting to be hung up. On the breakfast bar was a half drunk mug of coffee, and the milk had been left beside the mug. The iron had been unplugged but was sitting on the ironing board as if to be used again. Nothing else was disturbed and it didn't look as though he had taken many (if any) clothes with him. It looked as though Declan had run, and left in a hurry.

The landlady packed up all his things, and I took them with me. I left most of the boxes in the garage for at least a year in case he came back looking for them. The television found a home in my bedroom.

I called Declan's sister in Dublin to let her know of our divorce, and of his disappearance. I also called the police and reported him missing.

There was nothing else I could do but get on with life. My family wanted me to come home to Ireland but Austin was our home now and I was used to being a single parent, having been one through most of my marriage.

Single Parenting is a Lonely Job

I FIGURED THAT WITH THE SMALL SALARY I WAS earning, along with the bi-yearly money I got from the Thalidomide Trust, I could probably just about make it financially. I contacted the bank and arranged to have the mortgage put in my name only—and by doing this I was able to reduce my payments considerably because the interest rate had dropped from 9.5% to around 4%. I was so nervous of making such major decisions myself but once again Delores was my rock and she was able to advise me on what sensible financial moves to make and what financial risks not to take.

It was tough work as a single parent, and one with a disability at that. Even what you would consider a simple task like taking the children for a walk was extremely difficult and time consuming. I used a sling for Aisling that was strapped onto the front of me. In order to get her into the sling I would lie her on the changing table and then gently wriggle her into it, talking to her and making a game of it for Karl. I would sit her up and I would slide my own head through the opening and put my arms in one at a time while still holding Aisling. Then I could sit up and she would come with me. Getting her out of it again was a little more challenging and would mean I lay on the bed on my side with her while I wriggled out of the sling.

On the weekend mornings we would walk down to the local gas station and buy Karl an ice cream or some little sweets. Our walks were good exercise for Karl and when he got his first little bike he would cycle alongside me. It took forever but the weather was good and we were in no hurry.

One evening I was talking to John's wife on the phone and she said I sounded exhausted. John was the thalidomide guy I had previously met at an ADAPT meeting. I told her I was trying to hold it all together but I was constantly tired from everything taking longer for me to do. She told me about a small program that allowed people to continue to work and receive PA hours—the person co-paid depending on their income. As my income was quite small I didn't have to co-pay at all. I applied in person to the program the following day and was accepted onto it. Within a week I held three interviews and decided on an older lady who was training to be an Occupational Therapist. I think she was also intrigued with our little family and delighted to take the job. The difference of having a PA was amazing. Now we could go out to the park at the weekends without worrying about how I would change nappies. The PA could also push the stroller with Aisling in it if we went to the mall or anywhere involving a lot of walking. Karl loved to walk but if he got tired I could sit him on the chair in front of me. The PA would also cook us dinner in the evening and bathe the kids with me watching over the operation. Suddenly I was getting more sleep and was able to spend more time with the children. I was also able to take a bath or shower while she was there with the kids and not worry about something happening while I was washing.

My divorce became final at the end of April 1997. I went to court but Declan did not show up. The judge granted me full custody of the children but I asked that Declan be allowed access anytime he wanted provided he was sober. I requested that he should never be allowed to take the children away from the house unsupervised. The judge asked could I manage the children alone, but I assured her I had a PA and had been managing alone for almost a year now. She was satisfied with that and signed the divorce decree.

Over the next few months I became increasingly grateful to my attorney for having put in the divorce papers that I was not responsible for Declan's debts. I received a number of phone calls from people he owed money to, he had obviously given them my number. I told them I was not legally obligated to pay anything and they should go after him instead.

When Aisling turned one, my friend Cairn came over from Ireland to visit us. Delores told me that as I hadn't had a break away from the kids since we moved to Texas, that she would stay at our house and Cairn and I should go to San Antonio for the night.

I dropped the kids at daycare (Delores was going to collect them) and we set out. We did the tourist attractions and looked around the Alamo site. We ate at a nice restaurant while catching up on all the gossip from back home, and then hit Durty Nelly's Irish bar. There was a piano player there singing Irish songs, so Cairn and I got ourselves drinks and sat up beside the piano, singing away with him.

The night wore on and we ended up sitting next to a bunch of guys who were in San Antonio for a conference, but who were going back to El Paso the next morning. They were civilian workers from the military base there. After all the laughing and talking, we all decided to move to another Irish bar. Cairn played some pool there with a couple of the lads while I sat and chatted to a guy called Kevin.

When the bar closed at around 1am Cairn and myself started walking towards our hotel, but Kevin said he would come along to make sure we got there safely. When we reached the hotel, Cairn said she was tired and went off to bed while we sat in the lobby and chatted. After a time Kevin asked if I would like to go back to his hotel room with him. It had been such a long time since a man had made me feel like a desirable woman, and he seemed so kind and gentle, that I said yes. But—romantic as ever—I told him I had to take my battery charger with me. He got it from the room for me and carried it back to his hotel.

We had such a beautiful night of passion, it made me feel like a woman again. Kevin was older than me and very experienced. Him telling me I was a beautiful woman was the boost in morale I needed to let me know I had worth and value in life. In the morning he ordered breakfast to the room, and then he left to go to the airport while I left to go back to our hotel. I had him call Cairn earlier to let her know I had not been kidnapped, as she was sleeping when we'd left our hotel.

Cairn and I giggled the whole way back to Austin about our night out. I had never done anything like that before, but it was surely what the doctor ordered to lift my spirits and make me feel I could carry on parenting alone. That night made me realize I was as good as any other woman and gave me hope that one day I might find the right man to have a relationship with, who would love myself and the children.

Shortly after Cairn's visit, and with a new boost to my self esteem, I sent my resume to several disability rights based organizations in Austin. I heard back from one of them, and after a successful interview, got a job. The pay was much better than before, and now the kids and I all had health insurance. Before I took the job I discussed it with Delores. There would be some travel involved, but she said to take the job and she would come stay at our house when I needed to travel for work. Again, she came through for me. She was my guardian angel. Declan had not paid any child support since the divorce so I was happy with the extra money coming in from the new job.

Our first Christmas alone was strange. Delores bought the kids three toys each from Santa, as was getting to be her tradition now, while I managed to buy them two presents each. Aisling really didn't understand the whole Santa business, but Karl was so excited. We put them to bed on Christmas Eve, and then after checking they were asleep we hauled all the toys out of the closet in my room and set them out—Karl's in one part of the room, Aisling's in another.

Christmas morning was a little lonely, even with Delores there. I had bought her a present and she made sure there was something under the tree for me. As I looked at all of us I began to understand that even though their father had not fulfilled his responsibilities to the children and myself, we were all having a nice time and the children had their needs taken care of and were happy and healthy.

During the next year or so my neighbours were so good to us. We were always invited to neighbourhood events like the Easter Egg hunt, summer parties, Halloween trick or treating, and Karl was even invited to decorate a gingerbread house with the other kids at a neighbour's house. Delores continued to be very supportive and my neighbour Nancy, who was also a single parent, became a good friend.

The loneliness and sense of responsibility of single parenting was never far away though,, and was brought home to me one Saturday. I took Karl, Aisling and a friend's two boys to the circus which was held in a huge circular arena right next to the Children's Hospital. Aisling was two and was watching the opening parade from our seats with the boys when I gave each of them a hotdog. Suddenly Aisling began leaping around trying to breathe and I realized she was choking. I grabbed her and ran outside to the main concourse area, shouting that my daughter was choking and could someone help. One lady from the shop there tried to do the Heimlich manoeuvre while someone else ran for the Emergency Medical Staff (EMS). The paramedics who were on site for the circus arrived within a minute or so and one of them tried the manoeuvre another four or five times before Aisling's lips turned blue and she stopped breathing. I was frantic by this time but the EMS worker calmly put her finger into Aisling's throat and pulled out enough hotdog to allow her to breathe again. They put her on a stretcher and said they would take her next door to the children's hospital. A security man from the centre told me he would stay with the boys and I called their mother to let her know what was happening. Brenda said she would collect her boys and Karl and bring Karl to Delores. I also called Delores who said she would go out to our house to stay with

Karl while I was at the hospital with Aisling.

The next 24 hours were the longest of my life. When Aisling arrived at the hospital she was taken to surgery because she had tried so hard to suck in air that she had pulled little pieces of the hotdog down into her lungs and now they needed to use little tweezers to take each one out, as leaving them in her lungs would cause infection. Putting the instrument into her lung caused it to fill up with fluid so she was basically drowning from the inside. So she was put on life support for 24 hours while they pumped the fluid from her lungs.

As I sat there by her bedside I realized that I had good friends but it wasn't the same as having a partner you can rely on. If anything were to happen to me the kids would have nobody. I had nobody to hold me, comfort me or give me a break while they sat with Aisling. That night I was angry with God for me being in this position, but as dawn rose I felt at peace and knew how blessed I really was to have been given two beautiful children, to have been given a second chance with Aisling, and to have been given the strength to leave Declan and also make a better life for us.

That morning they began weaning her off the powerful anaesthetic drugs and took her off life support to see if she could breathe by herself. Once she could breathe alone she was moved from the Intensive Care Unit to a regular ward. She woke up shortly afterwards wanting something to eat, and within an hour was jumping all over the bed. My friend Brenda brought Karl to the hospital and soon both of them were leaping around together. The doctor discharged her after telling me that popcorn was the number one killer of small children from choking, with hotdogs following close behind. After that, anytime either of them ordered a hotdog at a restaurant I had the waitress slice it up inside the bun before it came to the table. That way the kids thought they were getting regular hotdogs and I had peace of mind knowing they couldn't choke on it.

KARL MISSED DECLAN AND HAD A SAD LOOK IN HIS LITTLE eyes most of the time. Then one morning when we were on the sofa together watching *The Lion King* it came to the part where Simba's father falls off the cliff chasing after Simba and is trampled to death by a herd of wildebeest, Karl suddenly told me that it was Simba's fault. I understood where this was going and I told him that it wasn't Simba's fault and it wasn't his fault that his Dad had gone either. I told him sometimes grown-ups do stupid things, and his Dad making the choice to leave was really stupid. I told him his Dad was missing seeing how wonderful he and Aisling were, and that one day I hoped he would know this, but if he missed out on all the fun times it was his own fault—nobody's else's. You could almost see the dark cloud lift from Karl and the sadness leave his little eyes as I cuddled him. Children are incredible the way the love unconditionally and even at that young age are ready to blame themselves instead of seeing the faults of others.

AISLING SOON TURNED THREE AND HAD BEEN HAVING CONSTANT ear infections. The doctor suggested we have her hearing checked and get an appointment with an ear, nose and throat specialist. A hearing test discovered that she was indeed very deaf and she needed grommets put in her ears to stop the infections. The doctor also decided that he would remove her tonsils and adenoids at the same time.

After the surgery, although Aisling wasn't supposed to eat anything, she was ravenous and was asking my PA for jam sandwiches. We gave her one on soft bread and a glass of milk, and she gobbled it down and asked for more. It obviously would take more than surgery to put Aisling off her food.

After the surgery Aisling heard things she had never heard before, such as the air conditioning unit outside her bedroom window, birds chirping, crickets making a racket in the evening. The television was much quieter too, and she couldn't bear anyone yelling close to her because it hurt her ears. Before, we would have to shout just to have her hear us. The first evening after surgery she came running out of her bedroom screaming 'Mom, Mom, there's a potato coming'. She meant a tornado; she had heard the air conditioner click on for the first time and thought the roar of it was a tornado.

Although I worked hard all week, my weekends were strictly for the children. They would run into my bedroom on a Saturday morning and we would all snuggle together in the bed—one on either side of me—and decide what we wanted to do that day. The local city pool was a favourite place because it was close. It was cheap too and I could bring in a cooler with drinks and sandwiches and make a day of it. There was a large park next to it with a playground in the middle and we spent many happy hours there.

One end of the pool was a ramp and ran from no water to about 4ft. The other end of the pool was deeper and people could swim lengths there. I taught both children how to swim by first sitting with them in the shallowest part of the pool and letting them splash around. Then I would take their hands and move into more water, holding them and letting them splash their legs. Gradually, over time, we would get deeper and deeper until I was waist deep and I would hold their heads above water with my toes and allow them to move like they were doing the backstroke. Then once their confidence was built up we would try a little swim together, gradually going further and further from the sides of the pool. By the time they started school both of them could swim a whole length of the pool and were not afraid to swim underwater.

I was told by a friend about a group called Parents Without Partners. I looked them up in the phone book and called. They were having an event so the kids and I went along. The organization was run for and by single parents who wanted the friendship of other single parents and who wanted their children to meet other kids in the same type of family situation. I knew that I needed to find some social activities to do with other adults and by joining Parents Without Partners the children could come along too. I met some nice people there but I felt like I was on the outside trying to fit in because some members would not accept me due to my disability.

I LOVED MY JOB. I GOT TO WORK WITH PEOPLE WITH disabilities and bring them to court to testify at hearings involving disability-related issues. People began to get more confident as they saw they could influence the political process with their own stories. I also got to work with Senators and Representatives at a state level. Every day was different and exciting.

However, my boss was a different story. She was a micro manager and would have to oversee everything. Even when we all put in our best efforts she would find fault. At one point she even denied us access to the board members, scared that someone would let them know how bad things really were at the office. At public meetings she would stand up and scream at any of the officials she disagreed with. She employed people who could not, for physical reasons, do the job the were employed to do, and then cause them to leave in tears because their self esteem had been destroyed; I couldn't afford to leave because I was the only breadwinner in our family. But I put the word out that I was seeking to move and hoped someone would be able to offer me a job with the same, or better, pay and benefits.

RELATIONSHIPS

ALTHOUGH I WAS STILL RAW FROM MY DIVORCE I hoped that one day I would meet someone to settle down with again. I didn't need a relationship, but I would have liked one. So I joined an online dating site called *Matchmaker* and put up a profile.

Although I never did meet someone to have a relationship with through this site, I did go on some very interesting dates. I met two good friends from this website—Reggie and Pat—and we are still friends. My friend Dawn was also a single parent and signed up to *Matchmaker*. We would swap stories at work about some of the losers who wanted to meet us, and some of the nice guys who seemed genuine but when we met them (not together) they were either mummy's boys, wasters, or had a variety of other problems. Sometimes one or the other of us would go and meet someone from the site for lunch and then have a giggle about it afterwards.

The best one for me was a man I met one day for lunch. I met him at the restaurant only to discover he had already not only ordered a drink for me (which I didn't like or want) but also then tried to order my food without asking what I liked—a control freak at best. I got out of there as fast as I could, after eating a nice lunch of course, and he insisted on paying for it too.

Even though I knew the chance of meeting someone through *Matchmaker* was remote, it was a fun and safe way of having something resembling a social life. I never went out in the evenings and by having lunch every now and then with someone I got to keep life interesting while still being able to spend all my spare time with the kids.

All the guys acted differently to my disability. I always told the person I had a disability before I met them; it was only fair if they wanted to back out of the date. But most did not back out. In fact, most of them ended up getting very paternal, as if I needed taking care of. They were fascinated by my sense of independence and some were intimidated by it. Texas men like to be 'manly men' and be in charge, but after my experiences with Declan there was no way anyone was in charge of me but myself.

STAND UP FOR WHAT YOU BELIEVE IN

IN 1999 I WAS WORKING FOR A DISABILITY organization. One day we got word that George Bush's brother, the Governor of Florida, wanted every state to sign an amicus brief (petition to the US Supreme Court) for the US Supreme Court to hear a case. The case involved two women from Georgia who had been living in a State hospital but who wanted to move into the community and receive supports from the state's programs. Both women had diagnoses of mental illness and learning disabilities. The state said no so the women took them to court and won. The state appealed and lost again. So now Jeb Bush wanted the US Supreme Court to allow states individually to decide who with a disability should live in the community, and who should be left or sent to institutions for life. Of course we were horrified at this and so a delegation went to meet Governor Bush. Having been assured Texas would not sign the amicus brief being sent to all Governors by Jeb Bush, the delegation left. Bush told the delegation that he understood fully that this was a human rights issue and not a state's rights issue. He said he understood that people with disabilities should be protected under the Americans with Disabilities Act.

However, a few hours later my boss discovered that Texas had signed onto the amicus brief. All my life I have stood up for what I passionately believed in. I don't believe that anyone has the right to talk the talk about something unless they are prepared to walk the walk and stand up and be counted.

My belief in standing up to be counted was put to the test. Around 40 people with disabilities, mostly wheelchair users, marched single file from the Capitol building to the Governor's mansion—about half a mile. Pandemonium ensued, as the back gates to the mansion were being repaired and were stuck in the open position. The people at the front of the march confidently pressed on through the gates. The officer in charge was horrified and called for back-up. The Department of Public Safety office (DPS) was located directly across the four-lane road from the mansion. From the back of the march I had a perfect view of the officers all running out of the office, jumping into two patrol cars, driving across the road and hopping back out. I began to laugh—it was a perfect comedy sketch.

The officers were rough with us, throwing wheelchairs onto a set of steps and leaving people balancing precariously with one wheel on one step and another on the step below. Eventually they had most of the wheelchairs lined up and they handcuffed the wheels of one chair to another to stop anyone moving. But some of the people on the march were from the militant disabled group ADAPT, so being veterans of marches and arrests they flung themselves out of their chairs and crawled back to the gates, where many of them produced their own handcuffs and chained themselves to the gates, which had now been closed manually. By this time I had moved to the other side of the street, but not before I asked Bush's head of security what did it feel like to work for a liar.

The man wasn't happy at my comment, and so he sent a police officer across to me to tell me I was under arrest. I asked the officer why I was being arrested and he said he didn't know. So I told him to find out. He went back across the street and spoke to the Head of Security before returning and telling me he had to follow orders and the man said I was to be arrested. So much for free speech! I borrowed someone's mobile and called Delores, who almost fell over laughing at my predicament. But she said she would collect the kids from daycare and stay at my house until I got home.

After the police realized that they could not transport wheelchairs safely—and the leaders of the march were demanding that, in accordance with the law, our chairs were tied down to be transported—they called in the local bus company. We were taken to the local jails; the guys to the county jail and the women to the city jail because there was not enough room for so many wheelchairs in either jail. However, the bus could only take two wheelchairs at a time and there were eighteen of us. It took almost three hours just to move to a few blocks to the jails.

We were all lined up in a row on a corridor and told not to go anywhere because they had no accessible cells to put us in. That's when the fun really began. I asked could I go to the bathroom, and seeing the look of horror that spread across the prison officers faces, everyone then said they had to go too. There was no accessible toilet in the jail and so we had to be taken down in the lift and across to the court house which did have one. An officer had to accompany each person to make sure there were no sneaky getaways, though the officers were very nice to us. A couple of hours later, at tea time, we were fed a sandwich, a banana, a little carton of milk and a cookie each, before we were fingerprinted and released. I had found the experience very funny, but the kicker for me was when an officer asked me could I jump up and down because their camera was not low enough to see someone in a wheelchair. I refused point blank but did think it was a funny story—one to be told later. We were released on our own recognizance, which meant that we didn't have to pay any money to get out of jail. I think they may have been a little annoyed with us when they finished fingerprinting and photographing the first person, who refused to leave without everyone else.

Next morning when I got to work, the staff who had not been arrested had bought a cake for my boss and I with bars made of icing on the top of it and a message of 'Welcome Back Jailbirds' on the cake. The kids were very impressed when I explained to them I had stood up for what I believed to be right and they happily went to daycare telling everyone mom had been arrested because George Bush messed up and mom protested with other people to let him know he had done a bad thing.

A few weeks later I was strolling through the grounds of the Capitol building in Austin when a Department of Public Safety Officer stopped me. He told me he had been one of the arresting officers and that he hoped

I hadn't taken it personally—regardless of what he believed he was only doing his job. I shook his hand and told him I was only doing my job too. I thought this was a very nice gesture.

I was always aware that the kids may be given a hard time by other kids over my disability and so before Karl started kindergarten I went and talked to the class. I explained to them that everyone was different—some people were thin, some fat, some tall, some short, but everyone has feelings. I let them ask me questions before telling them I didn't want them to hurt Karl's feelings by asking him about me but they could ask me anything they wanted to know while I was there. I got some great questions like 'how do you go to the toilet?' 'are you stuck to that chair?', 'how do you drive?' and 'do you live in a house like Barbie?' I told the kids they could come and play with Karl and Aisling anytime— and many of them did. In fact, since then our home has always been full of kids most days.

Each year when the kids' birthdays came around Delores took delight in making party bags for the kids to take home with them after the party. She came to all their parties and chatted away with the other parents. They all loved her being there.

Delores had a market stall in a town called Wimberley. The market was run once a month on Saturday. She did sewing and crocheting, and she made lots of little ornaments people used on their Christmas trees. One day Delores collapsed at the market. She was rushed to hospital and after tests she was told she didn't have a heart attack but her electrolytes were all over the place because of her eating habits. Her youngest daughter took to making dinners and freezing them for Delores so that she ate healthily every day. She cut back on the fast food to only once a week.

A few months later Delores was back in the hospital, but this time it was to have a knee replacement operation. The surgery went well and she came out of rehab with a walking frame. She graduated to a cane but she had a fall one day and it gave her a terrible fright so overnight she went from a woman who was keen to get to walk with no aids to someone who needed to walk very slowly on a walker. The surgery and then the fall aged her and I began to worry more about her. Of course she still wanted to stay with the kids when I was working away from home, but I always made sure my PA did extra time or that the neighbours checked on her on the pretence of coming over for a chat. The kids didn't understand that she wasn't as mobile as before, although her mind was sharp up to the end.

In 2001, just a few weeks before Aisling's fifth birthday, Delores called me one Tuesday and asked if the kids could come spend the night with her. It was an unusual request but as her granddaughter was going to be there as well, I agreed. Next day when I went to collect the kids I said bye, hugged Delores and told her I would call her tomorrow. I called most days just to check she was okay. When I called on the Thursday there was no answer, same on Friday and on Saturday. I left a message telling her I was getting worried and she needed to call me.

On Sunday afternoon the kids were at a friend's house when her daughter called to tell me Delores had a heart attack on Thursday and had been unconscious when the paramedics arrived. Her granddaughter had been with her so help arrived quickly. She was taken to hospital and put on life support, but as she had been without oxygen for so long her brain was damaged beyond functioning and so they switched the life support off on Sunday. I felt like all the wind had been knocked out of me. I never even got to say goodbye properly.

With tears in my eyes I went to get the kids to tell them their beloved nanny had gone. I don't know if Karl and Aisling properly understood about death because the only other person they knew who had died had been a little girl in Aisling's daycare class who had drowned in the family pool. At that time I had told them she was now a star in the sky and they seemed to accept that. Aisling waved goodnight to her every evening for a long time after.

Heartbroken, we attended her memorial service. Her daughter had compiled a CD of photos from throughout her life, along with classical music she loved. We were given a copy and the kids used to watch it over and over. Delores was cremated and her ashes were buried alongside her husband's.

A few days before Aisling's birthday Delores' daughter arrived with a box. It contained all the party bags she had made already for the party. I never felt more alone. I felt I had lost a mother for the second time and there was nobody to share my grief with.

LEARNING TO LOVE AND TRUST AGAIN

EVERYONE WAS TALKING ABOUT THE NEW MILLENNIUM. People were worried that computers would stop working, that planes would fall from the sky, there would be power outages, etc. I was excited because something told me that this would be my time—maybe a time of new beginnings where I would perhaps meet a good man who could love me and my children and become part of our lives. I was also hoping that maybe I would be able to find a job with better health benefits and better pay.

Shortly after my divorce I met a lovely man called Reggie. Although I knew Reggie thought the world of me, and I him, he could never get his head far enough around my disability to date me, but funnily enough we became great friends. Reggie's birthday was a couple of days before mine and so we always did something together to celebrate. This year, 2000, Reggie called and told me he was taking me somewhere special. It was an Irish restaurant on the outskirts of the city.

The place had been built in the style of a thatched cottage. Inside it only seated about 20 people. We had a lovely night. Reggie and I were always comfortable in each other's company, but at the end of the meal when the bill was discretely put on the table, Reggie said it was his treat. However, I sneaked a look and almost fell on the floor when I saw it was a staggering $250. We have laughed about our extravagant night out many times since.

I was in work one morning when one of the girls arrived with a tiny little kitten. She had seen it wandering right beside the freeway, so she stopped and rescued him. She couldn't keep him because she already had dogs and so was planning to take him to the pound. I knew that if nobody claimed him in 7 days he would be put to sleep so I said I would take him.

I took him to the vet to have him checked over and the vet told me he was only about four weeks old. The kids were so excited. They called him Scruffy because every time he used the litter tray he would miss. Karl would sit on the floor and feed him little bits of bread dipped in milk.

ONE FRIDAY I WAS PREPARING A TRAINING SESSION FOR the following week when my boss came in and began screaming at me about something I knew nothing about. She told me if I didn't like working there I should leave. So, when she went away I wrote out my letter of resignation and said a prayer that something would turn up for me as a job. That weekend I had a friend come with me to take my things out of the office. I transferred all the training manuals I had developed onto my computer at home, along with my contact lists that I had built up over the years. I figured that whatever job I went into these lists and procedures may come in handy. I wasn't stealing, this was all my own work.

On Monday morning I came in and went to my office. I took the letter of resignation and went to her office. She looked up from her work and asked if I had a nice weekend, just as if nothing had happened the previous Friday. I asked if she remembered telling me that if I didn't like working there I should leave. She smiled and said maybe she had gone a little over the top but it was a new week to start afresh. I slapped the letter of resignation on her desk and told her I was giving two weeks' notice. She was shocked and asked if I had another job. When I said no, she told me I couldn't leave because how would I get the money to look after the children? I pointed out that was my business and returned to my office feeling like a huge weight had been lifted from me.

Then the phone rang. It was my friend Mike, who was the director of another disability organization dealing with people in recovery from mental illness. He asked me if I could fly—I told him not without drugs or an airplane. Then he asked if I would like to go to Florida. I thought he was joking and said of course I would. Then he told me he knew how unhappy I had been in my present job and he was calling to tell me he had an opening and would like me to come and work for him. I went for my 'interview' that lunchtime. Really it wasn't an interview—we went to a restaurant, ate barbecued food and talked about my responsibilities in the new position and my salary. Although Mike couldn't pay me as much for the first few months, he agreed to pay the health insurance for myself and the children, so that evened things out.

Belinda asked me later that day to hand back my keys and leave right away. Armed with two weeks' pay I happily left and was able to spend some time with Karl and Aisling before starting my new job.

The day after I started to work for Mike he sent me to a three day conference in Orlando, Florida. A friend of mine moved in with the kids while I was gone and they only let me go after I gave my word I would not go to Disneyworld without them.

In my new position I was a trainer and travelled all over Texas teaching people about their right to vote, how the legislative process worked, and how they could make a difference to their own lives and the lives of others with mental illness by becoming involved in the whole political process at a grassroots level. I also talked to people about grassroots organizing and how people-power can be as effective as money power, which disabled people did not always have available to them.

One morning I was meeting with my boss in his office when our receptionist came in and told us her boyfriend had called from New York to tell her there had been a terrible accident there. A plane had crashed into the twin towers; in due course that it was 9/11 unfolding. We listened to the radio reports in disbelief, especially when the towers fell. All aircraft were grounded and the skies were very quiet.

That evening the children were playing in the back yard as I watched the news. Karl came and asked me what had happened and I explained to him some crazy people had flown aircraft into the twin towers and knocked them down, killing many, many people. His friend said 'It was the Muslims.' I explained to them that just because we were Irish we didn't want to kill English people, and so just because some maniacs had done this didn't mean our neighbours and friends who were Muslim would want to kill anyone. I was so proud a few days later when I heard Karl repeat this to some grown-ups in the neighbourhood who had expressed views on 9/11. People became anti-Muslim quickly and our Muslim neighbours even had to change their telephone number because of the number of threatening calls they were receiving.

Because people were afraid to fly, tickets were very cheap and so, with permission from my boss, I brought the children home to Ireland for 10 days at the beginning of December that year. The downside was that it put me in debt, but it made me realise it was a good thing to do because they got to meet and spend time with relatives. I realised how alone I was so far from home. I put myself in even greater debt that Christmas because Delores' three presents had to be replaced. The kids believed in Santa and I needed to give them the best Christmas possible. It might seem silly now that I would go off and buy tickets for Ireland, but a friend was getting married and I wanted to surprise her. She had originally talked about me being part of the wedding, as she had been part of mine, but at that time

I didn't think I'd be able to come back to Ireland for it. A week or two before we were due to fly out, I called her mom to tell her our surprise wedding gift. She told me her daughter and husband to be had decided that there were to be no kids at the wedding. So I called my friend, and much to my shock—because she too was a single parent—she told me the same thing. She even said I couldn't bring the kids to the church to see them getting married. I had been told that if I wanted to go to the wedding I needed to organize my own babysitter. Now, that was pretty much impossible from 4,000 miles away, seeing as she lived in a different part of Northern Ireland from my family and I knew nobody there. At the time I was very hurt because both she and her son had always been welcomed in our home with open arms and they had spent a few good holidays with us in Texas as well. When they had visited I had not given a second thought to taking time off work to give them a good time, but looking back I can see she probably didn't take into account the expense involved for me to bring us all home, or the impossibility of getting a trusted sitter from 4,000 miles away.

In Texas there is a law whereby if an absent parent has not had any contact with, nor paid child support for their child, then their parental rights can be terminated by the other parent. It made me realise that if something were to happen to me I didn't want to take the chance of Declan coming back and claiming the children and our house that I worked hard to keep. I went to a solicitor and had him go through all the procedures to terminate Declan's parental rights. Eventually I had to go to court and the judge signed the order stating that I now had sole parental rights over my children.

Coming back to Texas from Ireland for Christmas had felt so lonely. Although I had made many good friends over the years I had been there, they weren't family and people in Texas were more formal about dropping in. But my friend Debby seemed to understand my loneliness and suggested that her family should come to our house and we could have Christmas together. They were in the process of building a new house but the one they were living in at the time was not accessible.

So we had Christmas dinner with Debby and her family. Her husband had been given a turkey fryer for Christmas and was anxious to try it out. He brought it over and set it up in the garage. However, the weather had taken a turn for the worst and it was just below freezing point outside—this meant it took the oil about two hours to heat up sufficiently to put the turkey in it. We ended up eating dinner at about 7pm that day. Debby's mother in law was also there, and we had been sipping on her margaritas while waiting for dinner so I nearly fell into the dinner by the time it was ready.

Every year in our neighbourhood we had a New Year's Eve party at Gary and Linda's house, which was nearby. Everyone brought some food and drink, and Gary would take the kids outside and let off loads of fireworks. Gary loved to do this because his birthday also fell on New Year's Eve. It was always this time of year when we walked home from the party that I would wish for someone who would love me and the kids, and I also said a prayer that I would find a new job with better health benefits and better wages. Even though I had managed to keep our heads above water until now, I knew that if I didn't get a job with better pay soon, we would end up in a lot of financial trouble.

A few weeks later, as if it was an answer to my prayers, I was approached by a person who worked at the University of Texas in their Center for Disability Studies. She offered me the chance to go work for them. Although I liked my job I felt burnt out from all the travelling and training, so I agreed. This job offered great benefits and for the first time since moving to

Texas I was going to be able to have a whole two weeks off at Christmas with the children instead of having to put them into daycare the day after.

The first week in the job was very exciting for me as I got to fly to Washington DC to meet with some of our elected Representatives to talk about extended funding for projects we were working on in Texas for people with disabilities. I thought there would be so much to learn and so much to do but quickly realized that there wasn't a lot for me to do there. However, the health benefits I received for all of us were too good for me to quit the job and so I stayed.

SOMETIMES HAVING A DISABILITY CAN LEAD TO THE MOST hilarious situations. One day my car had to go to the garage to be repaired, so I decided to take the bus to work. The bus stop was beside the school at the other end of our neighbourhood. I walked the kids to school and then went to the bus stop. Four other people were waiting as well. In about five minutes or so a mini-van (people carrier) pulled up and all of the other people got in. I was surprised and asked the driver when the bus would be along. He told me he was the bus driver but was running late that morning and so hadn't had time to collect his bus. I asked how I was supposed to get to work so, looking a bit embarrassed, he told me to call the company. I went back to the house and called. The supervisor asked for my address and told me to wait for 20 minutes or so. Twenty minutes later a regular city bus pulled up outside our house. It was empty but I got on. Then the driver drove straight to my job without stopping at any of the stops. He even drove into the car park and parked right outside the front door of my work. Anyone can mess up, but this was a great example of how to put it right and make good customer relations.

I was now able to realise my dream of working towards getting a degree, and in December 2002 I took my first class in that direction. In order to achieve my degree I would need to take 40 classes, each one six weeks long. There were mandatory classroom discussions, questions to answer and essays to write. It would be a challenge.

Sitting paying bills at the kitchen table one evening I got a phone call from John. He called to tell me his marriage had broken up and he needed someone to talk to. I got really annoyed when he began calling me at 9pm every night, expecting me to drop whatever I was doing to listen to him. It was only when I asked where he had been when I needed a friend that I learnt his marriage had been going downhill for quite some time and he had been busy trying to save it. John and I then became close friends and sometimes he would bring his children over to play with Karl and Aisling. He wanted us to become more than friends but I wasn't interested—he was on the rebound and just looking for anyone so that he wouldn't be alone. I had enough problems without getting into a situation with someone carrying a load of baggage of their own.

I had been thinking about my friend Carmel, also a thalidomide survivor and wondered how she was. I decided to track her down. In March 2003, I posted a notice on a website for people affected by thalidomide looking for a friend of mine called Carmel. I knew she had got married and moved out of Dublin and for some reason I had been thinking about her a great deal lately.

A few days after I posted the notice I had a reply from someone called Eugene. He told me he had known Carmel all his life and I should email him for her number and address. I did and we began chatting on email, telling each other about ourselves and where we were, what we were doing, etc. It was nice to talk to someone from Ireland and I discovered that he taught mathematics at the University of Limerick and that he was single, and loved music and playing bridge.

They say that life begins at 40 but for me life really took an amazing turn at the age of 41. My life was on track in Texas. I had a job that paid reasonable wages and provided me and the children with good health and dental benefits, I was happy in my neighbourhood, and I had taken the massive step of returning to an online college to gain a Bachelor's degree so that down the road I could provide the children with a better quality of life by moving my career forward.

About a week after Eugene responded to my message (we had been talking via email and Instant Messenger a lot during this time) he asked for my phone number. It was around my birthday and for it he sent me a dozen red roses. This was really special because, the previous year when I turned 40, I hadn't even received a card from anyone. When he called me I thought he sounded nice, and so we talked on the phone for hours at a time. The children thought this was hilarious and would just roll their eyes and ask was that 'him' again. Okay, so there was an Irish guy interested in me. But after my experiences with Declan, would I want to trust another Irish guy? He could be telling me anything I wanted to hear.

We decided to take it all one step further by the end of April and agreed that Eugene should come visit us over the May bank holiday weekend. We both thought that if he flew in on Friday and back on Monday then it wouldn't be too bad if we didn't get along as well in person as we had on the phone. I told the kids of his impending visit and they were curious to meet this guy who called their mom and talked for hours.

I hadn't even seen a photo of Eugene so when we all went to Austin Bergstrom airport to meet him that Friday evening I was apprehensive about what he looked like. I knew he would be getting wheeled through in an airport wheelchair because he couldn't walk long distances, but that was all I knew about him really. There were a few tense moments for me when two old men came by in airport wheelchairs, but then the lift doors opened and there sat this good looking man in a wheelchair, clearly wearing artificial legs. We went over and said hello and Eugene stood up, the kids took his bag, and off we went home.

Over the course of the next couple of days we got on great. But one thing was clear—Eugene needed a wheelchair to keep up with us. He walked slowly on his legs and the heat of Texas was exhausting for him. So I talked him into ordering one and leaving it in

Texas for his next visit, if there was to be a next visit. I knew I liked him but I didn't know how he felt about us, especially when, over that first weekend, Karl went into meltdown over something. Really I think Karl was testing him to see would he run or stay.

By the time Eugene left on his flight home I knew this was the man I wanted to spend the rest of my life with. He seemed good with the kids and they responded positively to him—a hugely important thing for me. A couple of days later a dozen roses arrived to my office and everyone there who heard how we met began to believe that dreams really do come true.

Everyone in my office were academics. One day, shortly after the roses arrived we were all sitting in the kitchen area having lunch when one of the girls asked where Eugene had received his PhD. I said some technical college called MIT. She nearly fell on the floor, and after recovering she told me that was on a par with Harvard—one of the best Universities in the world. I began laughing when I thought of how I thought the Massachusetts Institute of Technology was a technical college and wondered why they were giving out doctorates. When I told Eugene that evening he began laughing and said he wondered why I was so under-impressed at his achievements.

Eugene was still working in Ireland at Limerick University, so over the next couple of months he flew back and forth numerous times to spend time with us and get to know all of us better.

He arrived back in the middle of July that year to stay until September. Then in August 2003, my friend Debby offered to keep the kids for the weekend so that we could have time to ourselves. We went to Fredericksburg, a little town in the Texas Hill Country and stayed in a lovely rural B&B. We did a little sightseeing and bought some presents for the kids. Apart from work this was the first time I had left them for a weekend.

There was a little restaurant down the road from where we were staying and so we went there for a nice dinner on the Saturday night. Right after dinner and before dessert, Eugene told me there was something he needed to know. I thought he was going to ask something about Austin, or about Texas, or about my family in Ireland or about the kids, but instead he produced a beautiful ring and asked me to marry him. Although I hadn't known him for very long I said yes. I felt in my heart this was the right thing to do. I was so incredibly happy—little did I think I would have the chance at happiness and a partner by my side once, let alone twice. I felt very blessed indeed. We called the kids as soon as we got back to the B&B and Eugene told Karl first that he had asked me to marry him and that I had said yes. He asked Karl was this okay with him, and Karl and Aisling were both delighted at the thought of finally having a proper dad. My friend Debby, who the kids were staying with, told me later she asked Karl why he liked Eugene and Karl told her it was because 'he makes my mom smile a lot'.

Eugene had to go back to work in Ireland at the beginning of September but before that we were to have a scare that frightened all of us. The kids in Texas go back to school in the middle of August, and the Parents Night was the next week. Eugene stayed home with the kids while I went to the meeting. After the meeting I looked at the sky and noticed it was becoming very dark, but I reckoned we were just going to have rain so I went on to the grocery store on my way home to collect some things we needed. When I was going into the store I looked up again and the whole sky had turned black—not a good sign in Texas. I got to the checkout and suddenly the rain began to fall hard outside. The wind picked up and the big glass windows at the front of the store blew in. Then CCTV cameras from the ceiling went whizzing down the store, the fruit and vegetables from the front of the store were rolling down the aisles, and the guy at my check-out was telling me to get behind the customer service desk which would offer protection. He pushed a lot of other people behind the counter too. Suddenly there was hail falling so furiously that if someone was standing right next to you, you would have to scream to have them hear you. I was very scared, not for myself but wondering what was happening to my family. Then the hail stopped as soon as it started and there was a deafening silence. We waited with baited breath to see if there would be a tornado, but then it began to rain lightly and a minute or so later the sun came back out. I raced outside to my car. It looked like snow had fallen. Everywhere was white—covered by an inch or more of hail. I jumped in the car and drove home. On my way through our neighbourhood there were trees down, one house had lost part of its roof, other houses had broken windows or other damage. I thought I would find our house in bits and Eugene and the kids injured or dead. When I got home the house looked okay but as I raced inside I still wasn't sure of what I'd find. But Eugene and the kids were okay. The kids had followed our tornado drill for bad weather, and had gone with Eugene to the middle room in the house—the bathroom—and waited until the storm had passed. The kids were really funny when they told me seriously that 'Eugene doesn't understand tornadoes are serious, he was laughing and singing the whole time'. He had been trying to keep them from being afraid but they thought he had lost his mind.

Eugene had to go back to work in September and would not be able to visit again until Christmas. He had already asked for a sabbatical but it would not begin until the following February. So those 17 weeks were very long for all of us, broken only by the flowers I would receive every couple of weeks and our almost nightly phone calls. The guys I worked with kept telling me that Eugene was showing them in a very bad light because they didn't buy flowers for their wives half as often.

Even though my friends told me I should do it, I never gave much thought to becoming a US citizen. But when I met Eugene I realized that if I were a citizen he would only need to hold a green card for three years before becoming a citizen himself, instead of the five years required of someone not married to an American citizen. Then we would be able to travel without complication. So I filled out the forms, got fingerprinted, was interviewed and informed when the ceremony would be.

On 17 November 2003, eight years after moving to Texas as a Resident Alien, I became a citizen. I went to the immigration office first and took an oral test on US government, history and general knowledge. The guy interviewing me only asked me a couple of questions before I told him I taught people with disabilities about the political system so that they could become involved in the process. Then a criminal check was done using my fingerprints. This proved interesting as I only have three fingers and no thumb on each hand, but the computer seemed to accept this was okay and I passed. The swearing-in ceremony that day was held in a large auditorium building belonging to the University of Texas. People were put into groups of 12 and then escorted to the front of the auditorium to their seats. When the turn came for our group, as we went through the doors at the back of the auditorium, a man told me to go sit at the back row. I asked why and was told wheelchair users always sat there. I asked for the person in charge, and when he arrived I told him I was becoming a citizen, not a second class citizen and therefore expected the same respect and dignity as everyone else. I asked had he ever heard of the Americans with Disabilities Act, which bans discrimination based on disability? Then I said I would go tell the news crew outside how disabled new citizens were treated second class to all other new citizens, and whaddya know, suddenly I was sitting at the very front, in a space reserved for the Homeland Security staff. It began to seem like wherever I went, even in a progressive country such as the USA, I would have to fight for the right to be treated the same as everyone else. It was exhausting fighting for my corner all the time.

At the ceremony everyone had to stand, put their right hand over their heart and recite the Pledge of Allegiance to the USA. Then everyone was made a citizen at once and given a certificate and a photocopied letter from the President. All the friends who had come to witness my becoming a citizen went with me to the local Irish bar/restaurant to have some food and celebrate with me. One of my friends had collected the kids from school so they could witness their Mom becoming a US citizen.

Shortly after I became a citizen I brought Karl to San Antonio in Texas so that he could sign the certificate that would mean that he also had citizenship. However, when he arrived back at school he had been marked absent, even though I had a letter from Homeland Security saying where he had been. It turned out the law in Texas didn't allow absences from school to become a citizen. We went to our local Representative and a bill was drafted known as 'Karl's Bill' that would amend current practices to allow for children to be absent if they needed to be in court, or with the Federal Government, so long as they were back in school before the end of the school day. The bill was passed into law.

BEFORE EUGENE HAD GONE BACK WE HAD ALSO DECIDED to move to a larger house, more suitable for two wheelchairs. So we looked and looked and eventually found a new neighbourhood that was being built about 5 miles away. We went to see the builder before Eugene came back to Ireland, agreed on some modifications that needed done to his existing house plans, and we signed the contracts. The house was to be finished around March the following year. Before Eugene went back, the builder arranged for us to pick our colours, etc.

On the appointed morning we went to a local store contracted with the builder. Without any hesitation Eugene and I went for the same colours and styles for everything for the house. Our appointment had been for an hour but we were finished in 15 minutes. This time, I felt so happy at having a loving partner with me who was taking an active role in decision making and who I knew would not let me down. This was how it should be.

I had loved our home at 12,500 Copperfield Drive. It was the place I brought Aisling back to as a baby, the place where I taught Karl and Aisling to ride their little bikes. It was where we lived when I taught both kids to swim. It was the place where we snuggled down on the sofa under a big blanket and watched movies together; where the kids danced along to the theme music of *Cops* in their little pyjamas before going to bed on a Saturday night. It was a house filled with love and great memories. So it was very difficult to make the decision to move to a new, strange neighbourhood away from my friends and support network.

We were told our new home would be ready for 'closing' at the end of March and so we began sorting through things to decide what to bring with us and what to give away. I was also planning our wedding. We had found and booked a beautiful venue at the top of a cliff overlooking Lake Travis. We were planning to get married just before sunset. An acquaintance of mine who part-owned an Irish bar in Austin arranged for a traditional Irish band to play at the reception after the meal. We were inviting around 70 people for a sit down meal and then the entertainment. We were trying to make the wedding as Irish as possible because mostly Americans just get married, maybe have a meal or a buffet and then go home. Even for the venue the idea of a band playing afterwards was a new concept. We were also inviting about a dozen people from Ireland and they would all stay with us—we would all squeeze in together somehow. The wedding venue staff thought we had lost our minds when we asked if they were sure we could only have the venue for 4 hours for the wedding.

In Texas, wedding cakes are not the same as in Ireland. They look the same on the outside but are filled with different flavour sponge cakes and instead of the normal harder icing they are coated with cream icing. We went to a bakery and tried several different cakes before settling on Strawberry with Amaretto.

I cannot buy clothes straight off the rails for the most part, and a wedding dress was no exception. I found a dressmaker who not only made my dress, but also a couple of nice little suits for coming back to Ireland for our reception there. She had never made clothes for someone like me before so it took a lot of time and fittings for the dress to look right.

SCARY SPIDERS

THERE WERE SO MANY THINGS I LOVED ABOUT THE states but having poisonous snakes, spiders and other dangerous creatures living there was not on that list.

One day a few weeks before the wedding Aisling came home from school and showed me her knee. She said a tiny spider had bitten her in the playground at lunchtime. There was a little green dot there and it wasn't sore so I told her we would keep an eye on it. Next morning at about 6am she came hopping into our bedroom and said her leg really hurt and she couldn't walk on it. When I looked I nearly died of shock. Her leg had swollen to at least twice its normal width and there was a huge, green, ugly, pussy thing on her kneecap where the dot had been. We got up right away and Eugene took her to the doctor while I went to work. Apparently the doctor decided to lance it but before he could, it just began weeping by itself. The doctor thought, from Aisling's description, that she was bitten by a brown recluse spider, which can be deadly.

She was given strong antibiotics to take and told to stay off her leg for a few days.

By the time I got home that evening Aisling, despite taking the medication, was running a really high fever. By friend Patti, who was a nurse, called in and took one look at Aisling before carrying her to the bathroom and sitting her in a tepid bath, washing her down. I gave her medicine to reduce her fever but Patti said if there was no change in an hour she needed to be in hospital. Luckily her fever began to slowly come down. But Aisling could not put any weight on the leg because of the pain so for the next few days she needed to be carried everywhere.

Three days later, after carrying Aisling to and from the living room, her bedroom and the bathroom, she was sitting in the kitchen with her leg up when it literally exploded. It didn't leak, instead we had to wash down the wall and floor after it blew up. Once the pressure was gone from her knee, the pain stopped and Aisling's swelling went down very fast. She was able to walk again but it took weeks to heal properly and to this day she still has a hole in her knee where the tissue never grew back.

We always knew there were dangers to living in Texas. We would often see snakes in the grass or on the streets on the way to the school but most of them were harmless. There were also scorpions, snakes in the lakes, fire ants (their sting feels like your skin is on fire), coyotes, and other dangerous creatures but we never expected something like this to happen so easily.

However, there were a couple of times that we had to call animal control because we saw a snake in the garage. The police officer would arrive, carrying a large pole with a hoop on the end of it. He would find the snake, manage to secure its head in the loop and then carry the snake off, at arms length, to his car. Then he would drive slowly to the end of the neighbourhood where there was a wood. He released the snake there, away from the houses. The snakes the officer caught both times were harmless rat snakes. As the area our houses were built on used to be farmland, it was no surprise to find these snakes. Apparently they lived in the corn and cotton fields and ate the rats there, so protecting the crops.

Our New Family

Dare I hope that this marriage was the right thing to do? What if Eugene suddenly changed and becomes controlling and abusive the way Declan did? Am I doing the right thing for the kids or putting them in harm's way? If it doesn't work out will I have the strength to walk away again? If we were to split up would the kids ever forgive me for putting them through single parenthood again? There were so many concerns, and yet I am happy at the thought of Eugene becoming part of our family.

My friend John, the thalidomide man I had met who had children the same age as mine, liked Eugene and some days both of them would go off to have lunch and watch a movie. Neither of them was working at the time so it passed a day nicely for them. A couple of months before our wedding I had a call to say John was very ill in hospital. I knew he had been under tremendous pressure from his ex-wife. She wanted more money from him that he didn't have because he wasn't working. She was married again and now threatening to take the children out of Texas to live unless he paid her more alimony. John was fighting her on this decision, and when I had seen him a few days previously, he had said he wasn't feeling well. Everyone had told him to go to the doctor, but he ignored the advice. He thought he was just coming down with a cold and that was why he had such a bad headache all the time.

Apparently his PA had left him sitting on a stool at his computer around 11pm one night. John had an early appointment the next morning and when the PA went in to help him shower and dress at around 7am he had found him lying on his back in a pool of vomit where he had fallen off the stool. It transpired that John had had a stroke caused by high blood pressure. John never regained full consciousness. His hypothalamus had been damaged, meaning that his body temperature was no longer controlled and his temperature soared. To stop the high temperature causing more damage to his brain he was lying on a bed of ice, but still was extremely hot. A few days later, just as they had his temperature under control, he had a second massive stroke in the hospital and died shortly afterwards. We went to his funeral service and met his family afterwards. His kids didn't really properly understand what was happening but they knew their dad was gone and were taking it hard. I was worried too that maybe thalidomide damage had been the cause and I began to worry about my own children should something like this happen to me. I visited my own doctor for a check-up and made lots of enquiries but I was assured John would probably have been prone to high blood pressure regardless of his disability and it was not thalidomide related.

On 30 May, the evening before our wedding, my friends and neighbours from our old neighbourhood arranged to come to our house while we were all at the wedding rehearsal and bring food to have a meal for all our guests from Ireland, as well as a few friends from Texas. After the meal I went to the airport to collect Eugene's only brother, who was to be his best man. I had been a little nervous at the fact he was flying in so late, but he assured us he would be there. Eugene had organized the suits through measurements given via email, but there would be no time to make changes if the suit didn't fit correctly. His other best man had been with us for a couple of days and his suit was fine.

At the airport I went to the information desk, only to be told that because of a line of tornadic thunderstorms between Atlanta and Austin, all flights were cancelled.

By the time I got home, his brother had called to tell him the same thing, but still giving assurances that his flight should land by 1.30pm the following day—a full three and a half hours before our wedding. Unlike in Ireland, and because this was not my first wedding, I stayed at home that night and had fun getting to know Eugene's friends and family.

Someone went to the airport for Eugene's brother, and they arrived back with him literally as we were leaving. The wedding was to be performed outdoors in a gazebo, with a contingency indoor plan if any thunderstorms came our way. One of our friends was usher, another doing the readings for us. Aisling was beautiful as a flower girl, with a little basket of rose petals to scatter along the path to the gazebo in front of me, while Karl looked so handsome and grown up in his suit as a ring bearer. Another Irish friend who lived in Austin had offered to meet us at the venue and do everyone's hair. This was an amazing gift because of the extra time and money saved from having to drag everyone along to the hairdresser's that morning.

The wedding venue had never hosted a wedding for two people with disabilities before and hasty alterations were made to the gazebo to put a ramp up one side of it and make the path to it wide enough for our wheelchairs.

An hour before the service, when I was getting dressed at the wedding venue, the skies opened and there was a tremendous amount of thunder and rain, but then just as fast the sun came out, the clouds moved off and the weather was glorious again.

We married just before sunset and then everyone went inside for a sit-down meal followed by a traditional band playing. Many of our American friends were fascinated at how the Irish performed their weddings, but by the end of the night everyone was having a great time.

Eugene and I stayed at the hotel there for the night, while everyone else went home. Our Irish guests went to our house and took Karl and Aisling home with them. Poor Aisling was bawling because she hadn't spent a night away from me before, except with Delores and she didn't want to go home with people she was just getting to know.

The excitement of the wedding was no sooner over than we were getting ready to come back to Ireland for four weeks. We had decided earlier that once we were married we needed to come back to Ireland and meet the families. Because Eugene's family is almost large enough to fill a county, we were coming home for four weeks in order to give us time to meet everyone.

Eugene still had a car in Ireland and we arranged for his brother to give us a small trailer that could carry the wheelchairs. We were also having a wedding reception in Portumna, Galway for all the friends and family that could not make the journey to Texas for the actual wedding.

We flew back to Ireland and spent the first few days in Newry with my family. My sister Anne and her husband Gerry got on really well with Eugene. My friends met him and they liked him too. Then we went to Bray in County Wicklow beside the ocean for a few days, before heading for Portumna in County Galway. In Bray the kids met Eugene's cousins' children who wanted to go swimming. It was a cold day but all the kids raced for the water. A few minutes later Karl only just managed to get as far as my chair before collapsing onto me. He was so cold he couldn't even walk so I had to carry him back to the apartment and one by one the kids were put in under a hot shower to thaw out and then taken next door to the hotel for hot chocolate. Our kids were in total shock from the temperature of the water—they had only ever swam in the Gulf of Mexico or the local pool.

We spent a lovely weekend in the hotel at Portumna and all our friends from all over the country arrived to celebrate our marriage. Eugene's friend—a priest—performed a wedding blessing that was really like the wedding all over again.

The day of the reception we got the most wonderful surprise. Our friend Davey, who I went to nursery school and then regular school with and was also thalidomide affected, along with his wife, who we had met in Atlanta for dinner on our way to Ireland, surprised us by showing up to the hotel for the reception. When we had hugged them goodbye in Atlanta airport a couple of weeks earlier, we thought it would be a long time before we saw them again. But as I came into the reception area of the hotel from being at the pool with the kids, I nearly fell over when I saw Davey and Karen checking in for the night. It turns out Davey's mother had died in Ireland shortly after we had met them at the airport, and they decided to spend an extra couple of days after her funeral to come to our reception. We had around 150 guests at it, with a band and a disco to follow. Karl and Aisling got to meet all their new cousins and had a great time getting to know the other children.

After the weekend at the hotel we spent a week or so in Limerick before flying back to Texas. I really liked the people we met in Limerick—they were friendly and helpful and I could see us living there. Eugene was very keen to show us around. He was not happy in Texas and although he never said, I knew he wanted to come home and resume his old job and life here in Ireland. I had some major concerns about moving back to Ireland. Karl has dyslexia, and could he get the help he needed to get him through school? Was wheelchair access good enough now to allow me a good quality of life with the children? If we moved back and lived in a village would we be accepted or would people back off a little because of our disabilities? Would the children settle there after having lived their whole lives in Texas, which was a completely different culture? Could we all handle the constant rain or would it drive us totally crazy?

Once we were back in Texas, we needed to make a major decision—should Eugene apply for jobs in Texas or should we move the family back to Ireland so he could go back to work? He applied for jobs at the Universities around Austin, but it was going to be difficult for him to begin again in Texas. Besides, Eugene was concerned about being so far away from his parents. He also had been working at his own job for 14 years already, so there was the pension to think about as well as the job security offered in Ireland. In Texas he would just be on a year-to-year contract with no guarantee of it being renewed.

So we sat down as a family and weighed up the pluses and minuses about moving back to Ireland or staying in Texas. The kids were delighted that school started so much later in Ireland and both of them, surprisingly, said that they would be happy to move to there. After much discussion we decided it would be more beneficial for us to make the move and let Eugene go back to work at the University of Limerick. I agreed to come back to Ireland because since we'd left, new anti-discrimination laws had been introduced concerning people with disabilities and now many buildings, the transport, etc, were much more wheelchair accessible. There was also an ongoing peace process in Northern Ireland, and for the most part the Troubles were finished.

But if we were going to move back I wanted to be able to drive the same type of van I had in Texas.

I couldn't go back to the chair being in the boot of an estate car because since the kids had been born I hadn't walked and now the muscles in my legs were not strong enough to keep me steady on my feet. I still needed my independence so the first thing we did was to investigate if it was possible to get a similar vehicle there and how much would it cost. We discovered, to our shock, the same type of van was available but where we paid $40,000 (about €30,000), a new van in Ireland would be more than double at €80,000. It would take a huge chunk out of our savings, but we could do it.

In May 2005 Eugene was dispatched to Ireland to look at 14 properties that we had discovered via the internet. He was gone 10 days and when he came back, complete with a lot of photographs and measurements, we finally decided on a bungalow in a little village in the West of Ireland, not too far from Limerick city and the University. We put in an offer and suddenly the wheels were in motion for our move. The kids were excited but there was enough time for them to get used to the idea without being too apprehensive about it. The home we bought needed some renovations—two bedrooms needed extending and we decided to build an extra bedroom and sun room onto the back of the house.

At the end of August, 2005, I flew back from Texas for a week. I saw our new house for the first time and fell in love with it when I picked up the keys. There was so much we could do and we were on half an acre so there was a huge backyard for the kids. I met with an architect to have plans drawn up for the work on the house, met with a company who modified cars and vans, registered the kids and I with Eugene's doctor, and spent a day with my sister. Before I went back the architect had the drawings complete and was ready to apply for planning permission. Now we just had to wait.

Planning permission and the actual building work would take until May the following year to be completed, so we bought tickets for June 2006. An international moving company were to bring everything to Ireland. We also contacted a vet who could see us through bringing our cat home. For our last Thanksgiving in Texas we invited some friends to share the day with us. We all ate together, and as the weather was still so warm, sat outside and enjoyed each other's company while sharing our Thanksgiving feast and having a few drinks. It was strange to talk to these friends about this being our last Thanksgiving in the USA for some time. Most of our friends were excited for us and some promised to come and visit, while others made us promise to come back and visit them.

Christmas came and as was the tradition in our family, friends who were going to be alone for Christmas came to us for their dinner. Pat brought his legendary cranberry and walnut bread, and other people brought other kinds of desserts as well. We had a lovely Christmas dinner and all vegged out in front of the television, laughing and talking for hours.

Soon it was March and time to put up the 'For Sale' signs on the house. It was so difficult to keep it spotlessly clean all the time in case the realtor called to bring someone to see the place.

In May we spent days sorting through the closets, toys, clothes, and furniture to decide what would come back to Ireland, what would be given away or sold, and what would stay for us to use for our last six weeks in the house after the majority of the furniture, clothes and toys were shipped. We had to keep the place immaculately clean, and get out at short notice when prospective buyers wanted to look around the house. I was apprehensive about moving to a little village in rural Ireland, where the people may either accept us or avoid us because of our disabilities and the fact we weren't locals.

EVERY CHRISTMAS I WOULD SEND A CHRISTMAS CARD and updated photos of the children to Declan's parents. I wrote to them to let them know I was getting married again and to inform them that we were moving back to Ireland. His Dad now had Alzheimer's disease, but his mother had always kept in touch with me. I would talk to her about Declan because I knew her heart must have been broken by him never contacting them again after we parted ways. As a mother myself I know how worried she must have been for his safety and it made me want to strangle him for putting her through all this turmoil.

IT'S STRANGE, BUT SOME PEOPLE ONLY WANT TO BE friends when the chips are down. Almost as if it makes them feel better about their own lives if someone else's life is worse. I found that with one friend in particular in Texas. She was a great support and friend when I was alone with the kids and struggling both physically and financially to keep everything together. She was there for me when I was lonely, and was supportive of me when I met Eugene but once I married Eugene and we had pictures and plans for our new home in Ireland, she stopped speaking to me.

Coming Home

By April 2006 my car was ready for collection in England and so I flew back for 10 days. I landed at Shannon airport and a few hours later got on another flight to Luton, England. A friend of ours came with me because I was scared about driving on the left side of the road alone after 11 years of driving on the right, and having different controls in a brand new car was also a nerve-wracking thought. The next day we went to the company who had modified my car, had a test drive and then drove through Wales and caught the ferry back to Ireland. Then my skills were really tested on the four hour drive through Ireland from Wexford to Limerick because the roads are so much smaller than in Texas, and although there really was plenty of space I slowed to near stopping speed passing through the traffic calming islands in the middle of the roads coming into each town.

Trying to direct building work from 4,000 miles away is not easy. We had one good friend who would, at regular intervals, drive out to the village and see how work was progressing. She would send us photographs and let me know if she thought something wasn't right. Then I would call the builder and ask why this was happening. I'm sure he must have thought we had CCTV installed but between us all we set up a line of communication that seemed to be working.

During the next few days I met with the builder to assess how far the work was coming along, and I was actually able to get into the house now unaided because the first thing the builder had done was install a concrete ramp at both the front and back doors. There was still quite a bit of work to do although now the extension had a roof and the windows had been installed, but the builder assured me everything would be finished by the time we were due to move back to Ireland.

I bought electrical goods for the house and talked the company into storing them for three months for me, I ordered carpet and tiles and arranged for them to be fitted on a particular week, I met our decorator and put him in contact with the builder so that he would know when to start work painting the whole house and laying tiles in the kitchen and utility room, and I visited the principal of the local school to register the children to attend there. During our visit I mentioned my concerns over the kids getting teased about our disabilities and so she invited me to come and talk to the children when we got back to Ireland in June.

Before I went back to Texas I visited Dunnes Stores and bought enough Easter eggs to fill an entire suitcase. I also bought a few other little presents for friends back in Texas who were very good to us. Easter eggs are not available in Texas and so this was a real novelty because none of the kids, including our own, had ever seen them before.

At the end of April 2006 we became a real family, even in name, when Eugene officially adopted the kids. Eugene had broached the subject with the kids shortly after we married and they thought it over and decided they would like Eugene to be their real Dad.

We went through all the criminal checks on Eugene —standard procedure in Texas. A social worker came to our house and talked privately to each of the kids alone making sure this was what they wanted and making sure there was nothing untoward happening with Eugene and myself. The fact that I'd had Declan's parental rights terminated previously meant that the adoption process was speeded up because the police didn't have to look for Declan to have his permission for the kids to be adopted by Eugene.

We were given a date to attend the courthouse, where a judge asked the kids if they wanted to be adopted. They told the judge yes, they wanted to be adopted and take Eugene's name. She signed the adoption papers and then let the kids come to her desk and play with the gavel just like they were in a real court. Then we went outside for pictures and all of us went for a lovely meal to celebrate.

It took a while for Eugene and I to become comfortable in our new roles. After being the only adult in the home for such a long time and making all the decisions myself, I found it very difficult to share responsibility for the children with Eugene. One day we had a row over discipline issues—I think he told one of the kids to go to their room for doing something—and I disagreed with him. He was hurt and told me the problem we had was that the children had one mother and two fathers now. Of course I blew it off and was really angry with him for even thinking that, but when I cooled down and thought about it I realised he was absolutely right. I was still performing mom and dad roles and yet expecting him to take responsibility, but only when I wanted him to. He was in an impossible situation. So we went for a long walk that evening, discussed the whole situation and agreed that, in front of the children, we would put up a united front so that they would see they couldn't play one of us off against the other.

I was to leave my job in May 2006 and so the week before that I took all the family along to have our teeth checked, as I had great dental insurance through my job. The dentist, after checking my teeth and doing the routine examination of my neck, told me I had a lump in my thyroid and should have it looked at as soon as possible. I couldn't see anything, and I was in no pain so I put it to the back of my mind until we moved back to Ireland. After all, if there was no pain or discomfort it couldn't be that serious, could it?

I was nervous about our move, but I knew Eugene would be much happier—he was miserable living in Texas. He was at home most of the time and because he was fairly shy with strangers had no outlet to make friends in Texas. We both felt terrible about taking the children away from their friends.

I was very concerned that the kids in Ireland would tease Karl and Aisling about our disabilities. I was even a little worried that, as outsiders, we wouldn't be welcome in our new rural village home and would be kept at a distance.

The week before we left, friends threw us a leaving party and it was a great night, if a little sad. Everyone brought food and wished us well in our new life. The kids had their friends all stay for the night. Everyone was on sleeping bags because the furniture had already gone by the time the party was thrown.

On 21 June 2006, Aisling and I left Texas for our new life in Ireland. Eugene and Karl would follow us one week later. It was a little like déjà vu looking at the house in Texas for the last time, having done the same in Ireland years earlier, never believing at the time that I would be going back there, especially with a new family.

My car was already sold but Eugene was to hand it over and collect the cheque off the new owner in the week before he came home. It was also Eugene's job to make sure the pieces of furniture that were left went to the correct people.

I was filled with mixed emotions as we left our Texas home for the last time. Part of me wished we were staying, but the other large part of me knew we were doing the right thing by going home to friends and family. I remembered the way I felt when I had left Ireland 12 years previously. I had been filled with hope and excitement and plans for a new life with Declan and Karl. I had wanted to go to college, raise Karl to be the best person he could be and I had dreams that Declan could have his own restaurant open by now. Although plans had not worked out just as I thought, I had still lived the American dream. In the time I had been in Texas I had single-handedly raised two children, bought and maintained my own house, worked to support my family, and was almost finished my Bachelor's degree in Criminal Justice. I had also made some good friends.

It took six months to prepare Scruffy for travel. There were forms to fill, he had to have a number of shots at set times, the airline had to be contacted and we had to organize a person in Chicago to let him out of his cage to exercise between flights. To top it all there was no guarantee he would be allowed to travel on the same day as Karl and Eugene because if a body needed to be transported, it would get priority and Scruffy would have to wait all over again until the next available flight. It probably cost more to transport him than all of us together, but we couldn't even consider leaving him behind. He was part of the family. Now it was in God's hands.

WE ARRIVED BACK IN IRELAND AND STAYED IN A HOTEL for a week. Seeing as we had to wait for carpets to be laid and the furniture to arrive, we spent the first couple of days exploring the general area. We went to Adare and walked up to the Manor — the weather was beautiful, as if welcoming us home. We visited Bunratty Castle and Folk Park for a day as well. Aisling was like the real little American tourist, seeing everything through fresh eyes for the first time.

The furniture arrived a few days later and Aisling, myself, and the delivery guys spent 12 hours straight unpacking boxes and setting up beds, dressers, etc. The carpet had been laid a day or two beforehand, and we slept in the house for the first time the night before the guys arrived back with Scruffy the cat.

Aisling had agreed to go to the local school for the last two weeks of term so that they could assess which class she would go into in September. I went to the school with her the first day and talked to the nine-, ten- and eleven-year-olds about having a disability and how we really were no different a family than any other. The kids asked lots of questions—both about disability and about Texas. I think they were more fascinated with Aisling's Texan accent than with anything to do with me.

My sister, brother-in-law and niece came down to Limerick for a few days to help with the last of the unpacking, and to hang pictures and do other jobs we would have problems doing ourselves. Of course by the time they arrived Karl and Aisling had taken to village life like they had lived here all their lives and once they had their breakfast in the morning, they were off to hang out with their new friends until we had to go searching for them for dinner.

Soon our house was full of kids for the entire summer, every day. Our children were a bit like stars at the beginning because of their accents, but by the end of the first summer they had begun to select their friends and the other kids had decided whether or not our children suited them.

Children are a marvellous ice-breaker. There was a summer camp that year in the village at the secondary school. Camp Bosco had been running for many summers and buses even brought children from other villages and the city. The weather was beautiful and so I got to meet some of the moms when we were collecting the kids from the camp. I made the effort to get out of the car and speak to other parents collecting their children from camp. One day Aisling came out of camp and introduced me to her friend Lucie. She asked if Lucie could come to our house, so I went to introduce myself to her mother and see if she agreed. Her mom, Christina, was very friendly and didn't have a problem with the girls spending time together. Soon after that we got chatting and she invited me to her house for a cup of tea. But getting into her house was hilarious because she had a couple of steps and I had to run a mobile ramp up them. It was so steep that we decided after that she would come to our house instead.

When the children went to parties I got to meet the parents. Those parents that I liked were asked over for coffee or tea, and so I began to make friends too. Eugene was happy that I was making friends so easily, and so he slotted into a routine of going into Limerick city to play bridge two nights a week.

WHY ARE SOME PEOPLE SO STUPID?

WHEN WE FIRST ARRIVED BACK IN IRELAND, AISLING and I had gone to eat at a restaurant in Limerick. However, we were both shocked to discover they did not have one single table that a wheelchair user could sit at.

In July I went back alone and asked to speak to the manager. Again I asked why they were not accessible and did she realise they were breaking several laws by discriminating against people with disabilities. She told me the matter had been passed on to their head office and was kind enough to give me their number in Dublin.

After having called their offices every week during July, August and September and being given the run around, or told the appropriate person (although I was never given a name for this person) would call me back, I got sick of waiting for a call from them. So I called the local newspaper and decided to begin a media campaign to make them comply with their obligations.

The *Limerick Leader* did a great article on how this restaurant was discriminating against people with disabilities, and from reading the article I got the name of the person responsible in their head office.

The man seemed a little taken aback, but then composed himself and told me there was no way they were going to spend money altering a restaurant for one possible customer. In turn I informed him I was lodging a complaint with the Equality Authority and I looked forward to seeing him in court. I then said goodbye and hung up.

My call must have rattled him a little because less than five minutes later he called back and apologised for the 'misunderstanding'. By this time it was the beginning of December and he asked if I would give him until the end of January, by which time both restaurants in Limerick would be made accessible. I was agreeable but told him I would continue to check the restaurant each week and if he reneged then I would go ahead with the complaint. When I told Eugene he laughed and said, 'You really are back, aren't you?'

The four months from September to Christmas flew past that year with all the excitement of settling in. Because we had not seen my family at Christmas in years, I drove up to Newry to collect presents and deliver ours. Eugene's parents are elderly but because his mom is not well they could not come to us. So, on the way north to see my family we stopped off with them and had a late Christmas dinner.

On St Stephen's night 2006 we went to the hotel in Newry to enjoy a few Christmas drinks with family and friends we have not seen in a while. I needed to use the disabled toilet, so I went but discovered the door locked. I knew there were no other wheelchair users apart from my husband and I at the hotel, so I knocked on the door and asked them to hurry up. Three blonde, non-disabled girls in their twenties came out. I was angry because it is only in recent years that wheelchair accessible toilets have been introduced into Ireland, allowing wheelchair users to go out with no worry about where to find one when needed.

'Why can't you use the regular bathroom?' I asked. One of the girls looked at me and said quite seriously, 'I'm sorry, I didn't think people like you were out so late.' I was shocked that people in this day and age would still think like that, so I replied, 'It's Christmas, they let us out later.' She smiled and said, 'Oh that's nice.'

Cancer

By the first week in July 2006 everything was beginning to look more like a home than a warehouse so I thought about the lump on my thyroid and how I should have it checked out. I found out then how slow the Irish health system works. I was told I couldn't get an appointment to see a specialist for three months. So Eugene called a friend of his who is a doctor and I got an appointment the next day.

When I saw the specialist he said he could definitely feel something wrong on my thyroid so he ordered an ultra sound scan which showed two lumps. He then did a needle biopsy to see if the lumps were cancerous. The biopsy was carried out at the end of August. The results came back two weeks later. I had an appointment the Monday after, but as he would be in theatre I was to go to the theatre reception and they would page him. I just knew I had cancer and spent the weekend worrying about whether I would be around to see the children grow up. I probably prayed more that weekend than ever before. But although I told Eugene about my fears and I knew he was also scared and worried for me, we couldn't let the kids see me being upset because we had decided not to tell them about any cancer until after the surgery.

The specialist was straight with me—if the cancer had spread he may have to remove my voice box. He ordered an MRI scan prior to surgery to get a clearer picture of exactly where the tumour was. He also wanted to see whether thalidomide had moved anything inside my neck to a place it would not normally be.

I had surgery on 2 October 2006. The kids thought I just had a lump in my throat that would grow and look awful, so they weren't too concerned about it.

I had seen people who'd had their voice boxes removed. The only way they could speak at all was by holding a thing like a microphone to their throat each time. They sounded very metallic and dalek-like. I would have no chance of acceptance at all if I was left like that, and how would I cope with raising my children? I was terrified when I went to sleep that when I woke up I would never be able to speak again. The night before the surgery was a terrible wait. I couldn't sleep the entire night, and one of the nurses who saw how agitated I was about the whole ordeal came and sat with me to keep me company.

I was taken down to the theatre around 11.30am and had the anaesthetic soon after. At my insistence, I made the surgeon promise that if he could possibly avoid taking away my voice box he would. When I woke after surgery I saw a clock on the wall in front of me. My first thoughts were that it had gotten very late—I went to sleep around midday and now it was almost 8pm. Then I tried to speak and was overjoyed to know my voice box was still there and I could croak. If it was removed I would have never been able to speak again. I didn't know until later that I was so ill from the surgery that there was a debate as to whether I should be sent to Intensive Care or not. As it turned out I was just taken back to my ward after being monitored for a couple of hours. Eugene had been waiting in my room all evening for me to come back and although it was close to 10pm when I was wheeled in, he was still there and looking very relieved.

After surgery I had two drains in my neck, one each side. This was to drain off any blood or fluid still coming from the wound internally that might choke me. The drains needed to stay in for around three days or so until the seepage stopped.

The surgery itself was pretty painless, surprisingly enough, but the relief of knowing my voice box was saved was immense. The surgeon removed my thyroid gland completely. However, because he had to scrape some tumour off one of my vocal chords, it was temporarily damaged, and it took several months before I could talk without sounding all husky—like I smoked 80 cigarettes a day.

Lying in the same position for around seven hours on the operating table had damaged a nerve on the right side of my neck or shoulder and now I had no feeling at all in my right arm or hand and little strength in my left arm. So much so that I couldn't even manage to lift the spoon to eat my breakfast unaided. I was assured it was probably the anaesthetic but by the end of the week when I was going home I still had no feeling in my right arm, although the strength was returning to my left and now I could feed myself and use my chair unaided. It took almost a year for the nerve to regenerate itself and the feeling to come completely back to my arm.

A couple of days after the surgery the results came back clear from the tissue surrounding the lump that had been removed from my neck. While I was still in the hospital, we sat the kids down and explained to them that I had had cancer. But it was all gone now, and although I would have to take pills every day for the rest of my life. The cancer was not going to kill me or make me sick. It was gone.

I was started immediately on medication that fools my brain into thinking that I still have a thyroid. Without the medication I feel tired, cold and put on weight. With the medication I feel fine. My big sister came from Newry to stay with us for a while after I got out of hospital, and although I felt tired for the first few days, after a week or so I was feeling well enough for her to go home. After spending the first few days not driving, I decided if I drove slowly and carefully I could manage. My sister and Eugene were both very were concerned the first day I decided to try driving. I wasn't going very far—just to the pub in the next village for lunch with my sister. I was going stir crazy in the house and thought that if this was going to be a long term affliction I had better start learning to work around having no feeling in my arm. We got there and back just fine—I accelerate and brake with the hand I could feel in and was able to grip the steering wheel just fine with my numb feeling arm. If I were to wait until I could actually do things like everyone else, then I would still be lying in a bed somewhere being bottle-fed.

Because I could not feel the one arm, and because the other arm was a little weaker, I was no longer as independent as before. I couldn't dress unaided for months, and washing my hair alone was impossible. Also, I could no longer peel vegetables by myself. So, having gotten a medical card in Ireland because of my disability, I now asked for a PA. I reckoned that if I had someone for 10 hours a week to help me with household tasks and a little personal care, I would be fine. Eugene could have done a lot of the tasks on a short term basis but it was very important to me to keep the roles of husband and carer separate. We were married less than five years, he was working full-time and having a disability himself he had his own stresses and worries without having to constantly deal with mine.

Christina, who had introduced herself at the summer camp the kids had attended shortly after we came to live in the village, and had quickly become a friend, took the job and has become part of our family. She helps me to do all the things I cannot do for myself—preparing vegetables for dinner, changing beds, washing and vacuuming floors, helping me to do the groceries and many other things such as some personal care tasks. Having her as my PA means the role of husband is still Eugene's without the extra pressure of also being a carer.

EUGENE BOOKED A HOLIDAY FOR ALL OF US FOR JANUARY 2007 before I had to go into isolation for radiation treatment. We went to Florida for one week and went on a cruise out of Florida around the Caribbean for another week. But again I had to fight for my rights. We arrived in JFK airport in New York and, before we left Ireland and again on the flight, I asked for my wheelchair to be brought up to the door of the plane when we landed. Having worked in disability rights in Texas for so long I knew the law said that if someone with a disability asks for their chair to be brought to the door of the plane then that should happen.

However, the person dealing with the ground crew came onto the plane and told me they didn't bring chairs to the planes and I would have to use one of their chairs. I was afraid that mine would either be lost or damaged—and if I was in an airport chair nobody would take responsibility—so I refused to leave the flight until I had my chair. The standoff had begun. We sat there for about an hour and a half and then I asked to speak to his supervisor. When she arrived she was a lovely lady from London and when I explained what the problem was, within minutes the chair appeared. She was so apologetic. She took us to the VIP rooms and then booked us first class to Miami, as well as the whole way back to Ireland at the end of our holiday. Of course the kids were thrilled and now, if we're flying anywhere, ask if we could arrange for the airline to lose or damage my chair so we can fly in style.

Cruises are remarkably wheelchair friendly. The whole ship was accessible and most of the ports that the ships stop at have ramps leading down from the ship to the dock. The little Caribbean islands are so small that it's a short walk from the ship to the closest town and the people were mostly very friendly.

We visited St Martin and St Thomas. On St Martin the water came right up close to the main street and the white sand met the side of the road. Eugene and the kids enjoyed swimming and playing in the Caribbean sea while I chatted with the locals and explored the little markets. It has always amazed me that people who live on these little islands and lead more simple lives seem so much more accepting of people with disabilities like myself than people who live in large cities or towns in other countries.

When we arrived back I went and introduced myself at West Limerick Independent Living Centre. Before long I was asked to become a board member for them. They knew I wouldn't be able to do a lot over the next few months because I needed to get my strength and health back first.

I had called Reggie and told him about my cancer. He made arrangements and said that he would come over in April and then we could celebrate our birthdays together. When we talked on the phone he told me he was proud that I had completed my degree a couple of months earlier despite all the health problems since arriving back in Ireland. I had actually managed to get a First Class Honours degree.

Although initial results came back that surgery had removed all the cancer, as a precaution in case some cells survived. I went to St Luke's cancer hospital in Dublin in April 2007. Here I had a complete body scan to check for any other growths anywhere on my body, followed by me swallowing a radioactive iodine pill and spending four days in isolation—the iodine attaches to any cancer cells and the radiation kills them.

However, the treatment makes the recipient radioactive and dangerous to other people until the life of the radioactivity begins to drop to safe levels.

I had to come off my thyroid medication for four weeks before the treatment, and I slept a lot. I had low energy levels, and was constantly cold. My weight also ballooned during this time. But as soon as the treatment finished I went back on my medication, and I reckoned that putting on a few pounds was a small price to pay for my health.

For those few days I never felt more cut off and alone. My meals were passed in through a glass window onto a table on wheels which I could then push to the bed. There was a television in the room, a radio, magazines and books, but no other people. Not being able to move out of the confined space was also difficult and meant that I was not tired at night so the time was very long. I had a phone but I hadn't lived in the village long enough to know many people I could chat to and the phone didn't allow for calls to Northern Ireland and definitely not calls to the USA. There was a bathroom attached to the room and I had to shower and wash my hair twice every day because the radiation was leaving my body through my skin. I also had to drink gallons of water to help flush it through my system faster.

Cairn, my old friend, came down from Newry to the hospital the night before the treatment began and stayed chatting for a long time. But apart from her I saw nobody all week—no point in anyone visiting, because they couldn't come near my room. The door was closed with a sign saying 'Radiation' on the door to ensure nobody came in accidentally.

Having cancer had made me realize that life is too short to hold grudges. With this in mind I wrote to my eldest sister and told her that although she had hurt me with her behaviour, life was too short to hold a grudge and I would be happy to try to mend fences if she wanted to contact me. I put my home number and mobile number on the letter and gave it to my other sister to deliver when she went home after looking after me when I came out of hospital. I have received a reply.

Reggie kept his word and a couple of weeks after I finished my radiation treatment he arrived in Ireland. He was only able to stay for a few days, but in that time we did a lot of sightseeing. Eugene was working and the kids were in school so one day we went to the Cliffs of Moher. Always one for a challenge I managed to go the whole way up the steep hill to the top of the Cliffs with him so that he could take pictures and drink in the view. We filled every day with going to see different places and one night friends we had made in the village came over and we had a belated birthday party for the both of us.

When I was feeling better I was asked if I would attend an International Independent Living Conference in Dublin and give a presentation on the differences between what Independent Living Centres do in Texas, compared to their work in Ireland. In May 2007, I went to Dublin and the next day, at the opening of the conference, had the opportunity to meet the President of Ireland. She was very nice, very down to earth and even wrote a little message for Aisling, who had asked me to get the President's autograph if I spoke with her.

Getting to Know You

During the summer of 2007 we went to Blackpool for a week. We were taking the ferry to Wales so the night before we travelled we stayed just outside Dublin. I was in contact with Declan's sister Jean, and arranged with her that she bring her parents, Betty and Charlie, to the hotel to meet us and spend time with Karl and Aisling.

Betty was very gracious towards Eugene and she had a nice time with the children. I was a little shocked at how frail she had become. She now used a walking frame to get around. Charlie was just happy to be with people but his Alzheimer's was such that he didn't have a clue who we were. That was to be the last time Betty saw Karl and Aisling. When we went to Dublin for her funeral in 2009, poor Charlie didn't even know who was in the coffin even though he was looking in at the woman he had been married to for 50 years.

BY SEPTEMBER 2007 WE WERE WELL SETTLED INTO village life and Karl was beginning secondary school. I attended a meeting that was hosted by Limerick Youth Service in the village. They were asking for volunteer parents to start up a youth club in the village for first and second year students (12- to 14-year-olds). I volunteered to be secretary and some other parents also volunteered for various positions, including a man called Ken McCarthy who I had never met before, who volunteered to chair a committee to get the youth club up and running.

Over the next few months we all got the club up and running, but over time, as happens in most projects, many people backed off so that after a few months there were only a few parents totally involved in the organizing and running of the club. Other parents would come and help out from time to time when we needed more adults there because of the number of children involved. We had two parent volunteers each week and that meant that any club business that needed taking care of could be.

Now in our fourth year of running the youth club in the village, the outlet has provided me with many opportunities to get to know parents from other clubs who come to visit ours, and to get to know more people in the village. I have got to know many parents through their children attending the club. It has also given me an opportunity to get to know the teenagers and through this they have become more aware of people with disabilities and totally accepting of our family. Although there are no children in the village who attend the youth club who have disabilities, the door is always open to kids who have disabilities as well as those who do not.

Thankfully my health remains good although I never did regain full strength in my arms after my cancer surgery. The children are growing fast and are now both well adjusted teenagers with lots of friends in the village. They both attend the local secondary school and I make sure that I am the one to drop them into school, collect them most days and attend all parent teacher meetings along with Eugene so that the teachers and children all get to know us. I have been told many times that once someone actually meets me and spends a little time with me, my disability disappears for them. That is a very special compliment to me.

This village is a tight-knit community of people who support each other through all sorts of trials such as death and illness. People here really care about each other and we have been accepted with open arms.

I have made more very good friends here in a short time that I can rely on, than in all the time I spent in Texas. I am at peace. I finished the degree that I began so long ago, it seems. Someday I hope to use it to get a job but for now I am content looking after my family, being a taxi to my children, cooking and looking after my family, and generally being a regular mom.

I couldn't be as independent as I am if it were not for my PA (carer). The first time I used a PA was when the kids were very little. Over the years the kids have gotten used to strangers coming to our home to help with tasks I can never do, such as housework or some personal care tasks. When we arrived back in Ireland it took a couple of PA tries before I found the person I hope is going to be with us for a long time. People may not realize what a valuable service a PA provides. Without them I would not have been able to give my children as good a quality of life as they have had. Although my neck and shoulders are beginning to ache and show the wear and tear of improper use I can still drive and maintain much of my independence because of the help I receive from the PA service provided. It also lets me stay in control of my day-to-day life—something everyone wants.

. . .AND FINALLY

IN 2011 IT WILL BE 50 YEARS SINCE THALIDOMIDE was taken off the shelves, although it took many more months before people were warned about the true devastation it had wreaked on thousands of families all over the world.

But, having read my story, I hope you agree with me that I have, in many respects, been very blessed in my life. I was born into a working class family and we had our share of problems during my formative years. But going off to boarding school provided me with a sense of independence that I may not have had otherwise.

Being a teenager with a disability was difficult at the time, but looking back on my life I hope it has made me more aware of what the teenagers of today are going through, and I have a better understanding of how to deal with a situation where a teenager may be unsure of themselves or feel different or left out. I can talk truthfully to my own kids about their experiences and similar things that happened to me at their age.

Despite the expectations of many for me, I have managed to work in several environments and I hope, in some small way, been able to make a difference for others with disabilities coming after me. I hope that just by employers getting to know me and learning that you can't always judge a book by its cover, that it opens doors for others with significant disabilities in the employment arena.

There were difficult times being involved with and married to Declan and his problems with alcohol, but from that relationship came my two amazing children who are a credit to both Eugene and myself.

Making the decision to get divorced and go it alone with the children was a very scary decision to make and carry through but it gave me the opportunity to form a close bond with both children that will never be broken. Being a single parent is a scary thing sometimes and it has made me look at other single parents with a greater sense of respect now. I would also hope that the experience of not having enough money and having to go without for myself so that my children were looked after has made me more compassionate towards others in the same situation and more willing to offer a helping hand where I can. I hope I can better appreciate the loneliness involved and why some people rush into other bad relationships, just so they have someone to come home to.

I feel extremely blessed at having the opportunity now to be in a loving, caring marriage to a man I know loves me for me and has no hidden agenda. He patiently waited for me and little by little has given me back the trust I lost in Declan. We share a bank account and I no longer have to check it to see if money has been going missing from it. In turn, I am never quizzed over what I spend.

We live in a village where we are accepted by everyone. The children are safe, happy and well settled. Eugene is happily working away providing for his family, while I am more content than at any other time in my life.

The initial expectations that my parents were given for me are long forgotten. I am not a vegetable, I did not die early but am soon heading towards my 50th birthday, I have had the opportunity to travel and have friends all over the world.

Looking back on my time as a single parent, I remember all the times when I felt so alone and then one of the children would make me laugh. There was the morning I came from making my bed, and as I came out of the bedroom door our kitten, Scruffy, flew past my head. Aisling proudly informed me that she knew now that cats don't fly—having hurled him across the room to see would he stay up in the air. There was also the day when Karl was about three years old and decided to leave home. He knew he could not go on the road but he resolutely packed his bottle of milk in the device for holding silverware in the dishwasher and told me goodbye. I watched, hidden, from a front window as he made his way along the footpath, down two houses where a neighbour had parked their car across the driveway, blocking his path. So, after thinking about it, he came home again and told me he would leave after dinner.

My children have been a huge part of my life. I fiercely defend them against harm or danger. They are growing up knowing they have parents who love and support them. They are turning into strong willed but compassionate people who I hope will make a difference in the world some day. I am a regular mom with a loving husband, a home, and a family; just as I had hoped as a young girl.